people who
made history

people who made history

ROY CLEMENTS

inter-varsity press

INTER-VARSITY PRESS
38 De Montfort Street, Leicester LE1 7GP, England

First published 1998

British Library Cataloguing in Publication Data
A catalogue record for this book is available from the British
Library.

ISBN 0-85110-899-7

Set in Adobe Garamond

Typeset in Great Britain by David Porter Text & Editorial,
Greatham

Printed in Great Britain by Cox & Wyman, Reading

*Inter-Varsity Press is the book-publishing division of the Universities
and Colleges Christian Fellowship (formerly the Inter-Varsity
Fellowship), a student movement linking Christian Unions in
universities and colleges throughout the United Kingdom and the
Republic of Ireland, and a member movement of the International
Fellowship of Evangelical Students.
For information about local and national activities write to UCCF,
38 De Montfort Street, Leicester LE1 7GP.*

contents

Preface

Everyone loves a good story, and the books of Judges and Ruth are full of them. There is romance and there is adventure, there is political intrigue and there is domestic tragedy, there is even sex and violence. But these Bible stories are not designed simply to entertain. They teach important lessons about moral and spiritual living. They enshrine profound theological truths. Subtly they shape the worldview of those whose imagination is nurtured by them. And, most important of all, they help to prepare the way for the best and most wonderful story of all – the gospel of Jesus Christ.

This series of expository studies began life as Sunday sermons preached at Eden Baptist Church, Cambridge. Subsequently the material was adapted as a series of lectures presented at St. Helens Church, Bishopsgate, London, in the autumn of 1997 under the auspices of The Proclamation Trust. I am grateful for the sensitive and painstaking work of David Porter who edited the transcripts of the original tape-recordings.

Although substantial sections of the biblical text are included, it will prove enormously helpful to have read the whole of Judges and Ruth before starting these studies. Biblical narrative poses a special challenge to the preacher, not least the risk that the intrusion of his expository comments may destroy the sense of being carried along by the plot. Reading the stories through first as a whole will help to avoid this.

Every preacher is to some extent a plagiarist. I want to acknowledge a special debt to the volumes on Judges and Ruth by Michael Wilcock and David Atkinson respectively, in the excellent 'Bible Speaks Today' series of expository commentaries published by IVP. The reader who seeks a more detailed treatment could do no better than to look there.

The underlying theme that I believe links the stories of Judges and Ruth together is that of history-making. Many of us today feel powerless to change the course of events. We are the helpless victims of circumstances and events over which we can exercise absolutely no control. These stories quietly urge us to be less paralysed by pessimism. It is, after all, divine providence that shapes those circumstances and events. And the God whose providence it is displays an extraordinary interest in the actions of apparently insignificant individuals. His heroes are named not Napoleon and Alexander, but Gideon and Ruth. Even his he-men, like Samson, have feet of clay. It is immeasurably ennobling for those of us who do not enjoy any fame and who possess no influence, to discover that we too can aspire to be history-makers.

Indeed, when the books are finally opened, it could even be revealed that the achievements of the Gideons and the Ruths of this world have played a more crucial role in the achievement of God's plans than have those of any world emperor.

Cambridge 1998   *Roy Clements*

I
Patterns in history

1

God's strategy in human affairs

Judges 1 – 5

Joshua son of Nun, the servant of the LORD, died at the age of a hundred and ten. And they buried him in the land of his inheritance, at Timnath Heres in the hill country of Ephraim, north of Mount Gaash.

After that whole generation had been gathered to their fathers, another generation grew up, who knew neither the LORD nor what he had done for Israel. Then the Israelites did evil in the eyes of the LORD and served the Baals. They forsook the LORD, the God of their fathers, who had brought them out of Egypt. They followed and worshipped various gods of the peoples around them. They provoked the LORD to anger because they forsook him and served Baal and the Ashtoreths. In his anger against Israel the LORD handed them over to raiders who plundered them. He sold them to their enemies all around, whom they were no longer able to resist. Whenever Israel went out to fight, the hand of the LORD was against them to defeat them, just as he had sworn to them. They were in great distress.

Then the LORD raised up judges, who saved them out of the hands of these raiders. Yet they would not listen to their judges but prostituted themselves to other gods and worshipped them. Unlike their fathers, they quickly turned from the way in which their fathers had walked, the way of obedience to the LORD's commands. Whenever the LORD raised up a judge for them, he was with the judge and saved them out of the hands of their enemies as long as the judge lived; for the LORD had compassion on them as they groaned under those who oppressed and afflicted them. But when the judge died, the people returned to ways even more corrupt than those of their fathers, following other gods and serving and worshipping them. They refused to give up their evil practices and stubborn ways (Judges 2:8–19).

In the month of August in the year AD 410, the city of Rome fell to Alaric the Barbarian. For more than half a millennium Rome had represented law and order within the vast boundaries of her empire. Now her vulnerability to the forces of what seemed like blind anarchy had been exposed, sending icy shivers of foreboding across the entire western world.

South of Rome across the Mediterranean stood Carthage, the metropolitan centre of the Roman Empire in North Africa. Not far down the coast from Carthage was the harbour town of Hippo. Soon refugees began to arrive there, staggering wild-eyed and shabby off the ships. They brought horrifying tales of the disaster that had befallen Rome. They told of famous palaces and gardens now reduced to smoking ruins; of celebrated senators murdered, noble families exterminated and sacred virgins raped. Barbarian carts, they said, filled to overflowing with plundered treasure, were rolling triumphantly south down the Appian Way.

Hippo had a famous bishop, Augustine. Some consider him the greatest theologian of all time. Like everybody else in Hippo, Augustine was distraught by the news from Rome. It was as if the world itself had been decapitated. They used to call Rome 'the eternal city'; clearly now it wasn't. Had Hippo been shaken by an earthquake measuring 10 on the Richter scale, no greater sense of panic and insecurity would have resulted.

Inevitably, people started to ask, 'Why?'

Some of Hippo's pagans superstitiously blamed the Christians, claiming that Rome had fallen because she had forsaken her traditional gods: 'This sort of thing would never have happened in the good old days, before the Emperor Constantine was converted to this new-fangled religion of Jesus.' And, to Bishop Augustine's embarrassment, some of the Christians in his congregation were tempted to murmur cynically in a similar way. 'What have the apostles Peter and Paul achieved for Rome? And what has been the advantage of those martyrs' graves encircling Rome?' Like the Jews who complained against Moses in the wilderness, Augustine could detect a 'back to Egypt' lobby gathering strength in the dark arches of Hippo's basilica.

His response was swift. He preached a punchy series of sermons. In them he insisted that it was not the peevish spite of Jupiter or Juno that had precipitated this disaster; it was the judicial wrath of God. He thundered from his pulpit, comparing Rome to the ancient city of Sodom; God had rebuked Rome for her hedonistic lifestyle and escapist entertainment. Did the apostle Peter die in Rome and was his body buried there in order to safeguard her idiotic theatres and drunken revels? Not so, declared Augustine. The world whose collapse they were mourning was not worth grieving for. Rome burned because it was necessary to force men and women to pause and reflect upon the ephemeral vanity of all material things. God had used Alaric to chasten Rome, so that the diseased flesh of her decadent culture could be cut out of the body politic.

They were very fine and moving sermons. But was Augustine right? Should we too be preaching sermons like that in Britain today? Was he correct to have made such a direct analogy between the fall of Rome and that of Sodom? Ought he to have drawn that line of connection between Bible history and contemporary history? Does history repeat itself in that way? Or is it only historians who sometimes repeat one another?

I suspect that many Christians' instinct would be to agree with Augustine. On the other hand, many academics argue that he was skating on extremely thin ice. C. S. Lewis was one; by no means unsympathetic to Augustine's Christian faith, he nevertheless argued that Augustine was falling into precisely the same intellectual trap as were the superstitious pagans he was trying to refute. Lewis called that trap 'historicism', by which he meant the belief that it is possible to identify a meaningful pattern in history.

The most outstanding historicist of modern times was undoubtedly Karl Marx who, in his doctrine of dialectical materialism claimed that he could explain why historical events go the way they do. He believed that he had discovered a scientific law of development within the historical process. The unequal distribution of economic power and resources, he argued, produces an inevitable class conflict that can only be resolved by some kind of social revolution. Though the revolution may change the immediate state of affairs, inevitably new economic equalities arise – so it is only a matter of time before new class conflicts lead to yet another revolution. Thus the cycle continues, said Marx, until socialism emerges. And the battle between socialism and capitalism is the final revolutionary cycle, heralding the arrival of the classless society, a utopian state of permanent peace and justice for all.

In his foreword to the 1848 *Communist Manifesto*, Friedrich Engels claimed that with his theory of dialectic materialism Marx had elucidated the pattern that enables us to make sense of the past and predict the future. (In fact, Marx had achieved for history what Darwin would achieve a decade later for biology, when he published in 1859 his *Origin of Species* – the book in which he first articulated his theory of natural selection and the survival of the fittest.)

Today it is generally accepted that Engels somewhat exaggerated Marx's achievement. True, some scholars still consider that he was right to see economic conditions as the primary engine of social change. But it is obvious, from the misery into which just about every society has been plunged that has tried to adopt Marxism as its political ideology, that Marx's theory of history must be, to say the least, seriously flawed.

According to the philosopher Karl Popper, the flaw is fundamental. Marx was an historicist; and historicism, for all its popularity over the centuries, is a huge mistake. The historicists, said Popper, think they have found a pattern in history; but no such pattern exists.

The force of this anti-historicist polemic can easily be seen. You do not have to be much of a historian to realize how complicated is the web of cause and effect that lies behind even the most trivial historical event. For example, Marx, in his obsession with economic factors, completely ignores the historical role that an outstanding human individual can play. According to Thomas Carlyle in *Heroes, Hero-Worship and the Heroic* (1841), all history is the story of great men and women (mainly that of great men, according to Carlisle, but then he was a Victorian). And who can doubt that leaders like Alexander the Great, scientists like Isaac Newton or authors like William Shakespeare have influenced the course of human affairs? Yet, according to Marx's theory, such greatness is always and only the product of the economic conditions prevailing at the time. Carlyle insists that such a deterministic view of history grossly underestimates the creative genius of the human spirit, and the freedom of the human will.

Moreover, even a superficial study of history soon reveals that occasionally the course of human affairs has been directly affected not just by individuals, but by what seem to have been the dictates of pure chance. Bertrand Russell in *Freedom and Organizations* cites two brilliant examples of seemingly fortuitous events that had a decisive influence on history. The first is the indecisiveness of the German government in 1917, when it was considering whether to allow Lenin to return to Russia. The grant of an exit visa from Germany to Russia hinged on the decision of one junior minister in the German government. If he had said no, as he might very well have done,

17

the Russian revolution would have taken place without Lenin. You have to be a very strong-minded Marxist to believe that *that* wouldn't have made any difference.

Russell's other example is from an earlier period. In 1768, Genoa ceded Corsica to France. You may think that was a very minor political settlement, if indeed you have ever heard of it. But had it occurred a year later, Napoleon – who was born in Corsica in 1769 – would have been an Italian! Which would certainly have made a difference.

So any theory of history must be able to take into account the cumulative effect of millions of such random chances and apparently insignificant human decisions. It's easy, then, to see why historicism lacks credibility among rigorous thinkers. Popper and Lewis are surely right to insist that history does not obey rigid scientific laws. It doesn't evolve according to some simple rational principle. History is essentially complex, chaotic and unpredictable.

Nothing is more dangerous than to think that it is not. Most of the acts of political fanaticism that have marred the history of the human race – particularly in the last couple of centuries – have been perpetrated by historicists who were convinced they had understood the pattern of history and that Destiny was therefore on their side.

But those who look for pattern in history are exploring a blind alley. No such pattern exists!

Or does it?

I want to suggest, though it is a suggestion that in current academic circles would be labelled highly politically incorrect, that Augustine was not in fact so very mistaken after all. I want to suggest, too, that the reason that Marxism has proved so disastrous to the regimes which have embraced it is not that Marx was wrong to look for a pattern in history, but that he found the wrong pattern.

You have probably already anticipated my reason for saying so. It has to do with the Bible, and in particular with the book of Judges. Judges is a continuation of the history of Israel covering the period between the death of Joshua and the beginning of the monarchy. The first section of the book (up to 2:5) sets the scene for what follows. It tells how the tribes of Israel, in the absence of Joshua, attempted to continue their occupation of the land of Canaan. At first they had some success. But repeatedly, we read, the Israelites failed to follow up the victories God gave them. Residual pockets of Canaanites were left all over their territory. God was displeased with this lack of tenacity and thoroughness, as was made plain to the people in a oracle given at Bokim. It concludes this opening section of Judges.

> The angel of the LORD went up from Gilgal to Bokim and said, 'I brought you up out of Egypt and led you into the land that I swore to give to your forefathers. I said, "I will never break my covenant with you, and you shall not make a covenant with the people of this land, but you shall break down their altars." Yet you have disobeyed me. Why have you done this? Now therefore I tell you that I will not drive them out before you; they will be thorns in your sides and their gods will be a snare to you' (2:1–3).

It is not clear whether the 'angel of the LORD' was a supernatural figure or a human being. The Hebrew word for 'angel' means simply 'messenger'; it can be used for either human or supernatural, angelic emissaries. I suspect that

19

in this case, as in other angelic visitations later in this book, the divine message was delivered by an unspecified prophet resident in this case at the shrine of Gilgal. But it doesn't really matter whether my suspicion is right. The point is, God regarded the failure of the Israelites to drive out the Canaanite peoples, who had occupied the land before they arrived, as a breach of his covenant with them. The Canaanites were pagans; so their presence posed a spiritual as well as a military threat to Israel's future.

Explaining the pattern

The next section of Judges (2:5 – 3:6) spells this out. It elucidates for us the pattern that history is going to follow during the period of Judges, and it offers us a theological explanation for it. We are told in the opening paragraphs (2:8–9) that Joshua was dead. Once his generation had passed, moral deterioration set in among the Israelites. They began to flirt with the pagan idolatry that they had foolishly allowed to remain in their midst, and this brought about a downturn in their military fortunes (2:10–15). But it is at precisely this point that the distinctive feature of the pattern of history, which this book wants to describe to us, becomes apparent: 'Then the LORD raised up judges, who saved them out of the hands of these raiders' (2:16).

The judges from whom the whole book takes its name were not, generally speaking, judicial figures at all. They were charismatically endowed military leaders. We shall meet several of them; here, let us simply note that any respite that the emergence of one of these judges brought to the oppressed Israelites was always short-lived. 'Yet they would not listen to their judges ... they quickly turned from the way in which their fathers had walked ...' (2:17). So although whenever the Lord raised up a judge for them, he was with them and saved them out of the hands of their enemies as long as the judge lived, when the judge died the situation went back to being perhaps even worse than it was at the start.

So the pattern emerges: a downward spiral, in which for every step Israel takes forward she seems to take two backwards. Eventually, says the sacred historian, 'The LORD was very angry with Israel and said, "Because this nation has violated the covenant that I laid down for their forefathers and has not listened to me, I will no longer drive out before them any of the nations Joshua left when he died"' (2:20). God became so exasperated with Israel's persistent backsliding that he decided to take away the possibility of achieving military security within her borders altogether. Instead, the Canaanite peoples were to remain, a permanent source of spiritual testing – which the Israelites invariably failed to pass. 'The Israelites lived among the Canaanites, Hittites, Amorites, Perizzites, Hivites and Jebusites. They took their daughters in marriage and gave their own daughters to their sons, and served their gods.'

Othniel, a model judge

Othniel is the first of the judges about whom the book of Judges tells us. His story is unusual, largely because it has no unusual features. As we shall see, almost all the judges are highly individualistic, with very distinctive elements in their stories. But our author tells us nothing interesting about Othniel at all.

21

I suggest that this is quite deliberate, for Othniel's story functions as a model or paradigm for all the judges. It comprises a cycle of seven stages; and here is the pattern.

1. **A State of Spiritual Apostasy (3:7)** – 'The Israelites did evil in the eyes of the LORD; they forgot the LORD their God and served the Baals.'
2. **A Period of Military Oppression (3:8)** – 'The anger of the LORD burned against Israel so that he sold them into the hands of Cushan-Rishathaim king of Aram Naharaim.'
3. **An Appeal to God in their Distress (3:9)** – 'They cried out to the LORD.'
4. **The Appearance of a Spirit-Filled Saviour (3:9)** – as a result the Lord 'raised up for them a deliverer, Othniel son of Kenaz'.
5. **Victory Over the Enemy (3:10)** – 'The Spirit of the LORD came upon him.' He went to war, and the king of Aram was overpowered by Othniel.
6. **Temporary Peace (3:11)** – 'The land had peace for forty years.'
7. **The Saviour Dies (3:11)** – And so the cycle begins all over again.

Here then is the pattern in history of which I spoke. It is a pattern that we observe again and again in this book. Not all the stories of all the judges explicitly display all seven of these stages, but all contain some of them. Othniel represents the pattern in its simplest and least embroidered form. Our author gives us very little information about him as an individual, because he wants to achieve that simplicity. We need have no doubt that he had access to further information that he could have used

22

here; he has already used it back in 1:9–15, rather than here, so as not to sacrifice the simplicity of this initial paradigm in chapter 3.

Ehud, Deborah and Shamgar

He goes on to recount two more turns of the spiral: Ehud (3:12–30), and Deborah (4 – 5); a man called Shamgar is also mentioned in passing (3:31). In the case of Ehud and Deborah's the pattern is followed; so precisely that some scholars question the historical accuracy of our author's work simply because it is followed so pedantically: 'Isn't he just an historicist like Marx, who has a theory about how history should go, and tailors his reporting of the facts so that it conforms to it?' They suggest that the pattern we have identified has become a kind of Procrustean bed, to fit which he cuts every story.

I would reject that criticism of our author. He may be an historicist of sorts, in that he sees meaning in events; but the pattern he describes is a much more subtle and plausible one than that described by Marx. The guiding hand behind this pattern is not some inexorable, quasi-scientific law of historical evolution. It is the hand of a personal God, who is dealing with us human beings in a thoroughly personal fashion. There is no hint here of fate bearing events on a remorseless and unalterable tide. Our author is convinced that history is in the hands of a good and just sovereign.

So if there is a pattern that can be observed, it's because he is dependable and consistent in his dealings with us. He is victim to no fickle whims. Like a perfect husband, he is utterly faithful to his promises; like a perfect judge, he is utterly consistent in his verdicts. But there is nothing mechanical or fatalistic about his decrees. He is a personal God, and he displays personal freedom in his actions.

One of his main goal, in his ordering of the historical process is to teach his people this truth about his personal character.

Lessons from history

The book of Judges indicates that we can see that God implements his strategy for human history in various ways.

God's freedom of action, and ours

One way is by injecting a deliberate air of unpredictability into the pattern. Do you notice the intervals of time between the cycles outlined in chapters 3–5? There's no discernible pattern there. Oppression: eight years. Peace: forty years. Oppression: eighteen years. Peace: eighty years. Oppression: twenty years. Peace: forty years. The people had to wait for a long while, and for an unspecified and indeterminate number of years at that, before God intervened to save them. And the duration of the peace that follows is variable too.

If you think about it, that is the way it had to be. In one episode of the television science-fiction series *Red Dwarf*, the space travellers visit a penal colony on some distant asteroid. Superficially it seems to be a most enlightened place, an open prison if ever there was one. There are no cells, no locked doors, so sadistic warders. Instead, the colony is surveyed by a highly sensitive and sophisticated computer system that constantly monitors all human activity. It immediately detects any misdemeanour or crime perpetrated by the inmates, and instantaneously administers a painful punishment.

The travellers quickly discover there is no way to evade the vigilance of this perpetual nemesis. As a result, whether from conscious fear or from Pavlovian conditioning, behaviour in the colony has become highly controlled and conformist. As may be readily imagined, it is also a totally inhuman place. The regime of immediate and inescapable retribution has the effect of destroying all personal freedom far more radically than prison bars ever could.

When the travellers eventually leave the penal colony they draw an interesting moral from what they have seen. They conclude that it is necessary for there to be a time lag between crime and punishment. Furthermore, the time lag must be of indeterminate duration. Otherwise, there is no freedom to sin; and if there is no freedom to sin, there is no freedom at all.

That is exactly what we see exemplified in God's dealings with his people in the book of Judges. He wants to teach them that there is a connection between moral behaviour and divine blessing. But he wants to teach them this in a way that preserves their human freedom. Hence the erratic time lags between the cycles of the pattern. God enjoys personal freedom of action, and he grants the same precious gift of personal freedom of action to us.

Individuals as God's key agents

According to Marx, the pattern of history is so rigid that

no individual can have any ultimate effect on events. Events follow the dictates of dialectical materialism whether or not Lenin is there to help the revolution.

But our author is not so indifferent to the historical contribution of great leaders. On the contrary, he sees it as part of the pattern. God chooses to raise up such individuals regularly and achieves his saving purpose through them. And what eccentric and unexpected individuals they sometimes are; and what eccentric and unexpected means these unexpected individuals sometimes use!

Take Ehud, whom we meet in 3:12. The New International Version says he was 'a left-handed man' (3:15). The Hebrew is a little less specific; it simply says he had some kind of physical impediment. Later events make it clear that the only good arm Ehud had was his left one. I suspect that his handicap was much more crippling than simple left-handedness. Only that, I think, explains how Eglon, king of Moab, was prepared to hold private counsel with him in the absence of his usual bodyguards.

Quite frankly, Ehud does not strike one as a typical super-hero. He assassinates Eglon with Machiavellian cunning. He hides a specially prepared short sword on his right-hand side, where swords were not normally worn, and thrusts it into his victim's lower body, puncturing the bowel. That at least seems to be the implication of the rather obscurely scatological reference in the Hebrew text of 3:22.

It's a colourful story, this; full of human interest and unexpected twists! But thus the divine pattern was achieved, and Israel for a while was delivered from her oppressor. Yet, I think you'll agree, not in a way that suggests some mechanical fate is at work.

The same is true of the brief reference to Shamgar in

3:31. He was a warrior whose exploit was notable not for left-handed stealth but for bizarre weaponry; he killed 600 Philistines with some kind of ill-defined agricultural implement. Our translation calls it an ox-goad. Whatever it was, it wasn't a conventional weapon of personal combat. Perhaps we are to draw the conclusion that the Philistines had disarmed the population of the territory they had conquered, so ox-goads and the like were the only weapons someone like Shamgar could improvise. Even more unusually, Shamgar was almost certainly not even an Israelite. His name is probably Hurrian, not Hebrew. That may explain why our author does not list him as one of the judges. Again, he picks out an anomaly in the pattern, disrupting its normal flow. Once again, God is doing his stuff, but not in a way that gives one confidence to make future predictions.

Even more is that the case with the third judge in this series of cycles, who (wonder of wonders, in a culture so unashamedly patriarchal!) is a woman. Indeed, not only is Deborah a woman; but so too is the person who, in the providence of God, slays the cruel Canaanite general Sisera who is oppressing Israel with his 900 iron chariots – the non-Israelite Jael, wife of Heber the Kenite. Again, the story in chapter 4 is a macabre one. We're not told whether Jael drove the tent-peg through the temple of the sleeping general with her left hand or her right, but again, it's a very unusual kind of incident.

Do you see what I mean, then, when I say that though the book of Judges clearly believes there is a pattern in history, it is a very different kind of pattern from that proposed by Marx? It is full of space. Space for human eccentricity; space for the unexpected surprise. It is the sort of pattern that Israel could recognize with the benefit of hindsight, but never presume upon in any crisis. For it is a pattern drawn by a personal God who acts consistently in history, but never in such a way as to encourage fatalism or complacency.

That, I suggest, is the kind of pattern that the Bible encourages us to look for in our history too. It is the kind of pattern upon which Augustine was commenting.

Lessons for today

Of course, the history of Old Testament Israel and that of modern Britain are fundamentally different. Old Testament Israel, according to the Bible, was the chosen people of God. The reason God acted so reliably and frequently in the history of Israel was that he had a special covenant with her that he was honour-bound to keep. However, it is possible to see this pattern of history, which we've discovered in the book of Judges, in other areas. We can see the same kind of pattern in our own lives, and in events of our own days.

God is in command

This pattern teaches us, first, that God is in sovereign control of all history.

When it comes to the period of the judges, of course, we have the good fortune of possessing the book of Judges, a book written by a prophet given divine authority and inspiration to interpret events. Nobody can comment infallibly and authoritatively in that way upon events today, but that does not mean the pattern is not there. We may not always be able to trace God's hand,

28

because we do not have an interpretative, prophetic word to enable us to do so. His strategies in human history are often very inscrutable. But the book of Judges teaches us this pattern, because it wants us to know we can always trust God's heart. As Paul assures us: 'We know that in all things God works for the good of those who love him, who have been called according to his purpose' (Romans 8:28). In our day and generation, it is enormously important to teach once again this biblical doctrine of providence.

Many people exist in a state of meaninglessness. They feel that events go nowhere and that there is no pattern of things. Many others turn to superstition, believe in fate, go to New Age books or consult the old lady down the road who looks at a crystal, to try to reclaim some kind of control over their lives.

The biblical view of providence as we find it in the book of Judges is hugely important to human beings like us, adrift in the sea of time as we are, if we are to have any kind of assurance or peace of mind.

Judgment follows human sin

This pattern teaches secondly that human sin will issue, sooner or later, in judgment, and often that judgment will be temporal in the here-and-now, as well as eternal in the hereafter. Again it is Paul who talks about the wrath of God being revealed (present tense) against all the godlessness and unrighteousness of the human race (Romans 1:18). So when we see disaster befall a nation, it is not inappropriate to draw attention as Augustine did to the element of divine chastening, warning and retribution inherent in the situation.

29

In the Old Testament we find the prophets doing this regularly; not just for Israel, but for the pagan nations too. Jonah, classically, was sent to Nineveh, a pagan city, with just such an interpretation of events to offer. Jesus himself interpreted a disaster of his own day in this fashion; when the tower of Siloam fell he said it was a sign of divine judgment against the world. Interestingly, he was careful not to individualize that judgment, as if those who perished were more guilty than anybody else. He specifically denied that, saying instead that such events are to be interpreted as general pointers to the coming wrath. They are evidence that God is angry with the world. They are chastening warnings (cf. Luke 13:4).

'We have learned nothing from history'

> What experience and history teach is this – that nations and governments have never learned anything from history, or acted upon any lessons they might have drawn from it.

Georg Hegel's famous observation may serve as a summary of the third, somewhat sadder, lesson that the pattern in the book of Judges teaches us.

You would have thought that after three cycles of apostasy and judgment, Israel would begin to get the message. But the book of Judges goes on to describe how the spiral of decadence continued down and down.

Marx, by contrast, was an optimist. He believed that history was making progress towards a glorious man-made utopia of the future. Some Christians, called post-millennialists, entertain similar hopes. But neither the book of Judges nor the book of Revelation really gives

30

us solid ground for that kind of optimism today. Human beings are inveterate sinners, and as a result we must expect that evil will wax worse and worse and that there will be 'wars and rumours of wars' until the end of time. In fact, the view of history espoused by the book of Revelation is very similar to that of the book of Judges — a downward, spiralling motion.

Many historians, of course, have observed this downward spiralling of history and built their secular histories around such a theory. That is how in the ancient world Hesiod the Greek historian interpreted the history of Greece. Every twist of Greek history was a movement further and further away from the classical age. If you know anything of Chinese historiography, a similar kind of view of history is found there. Every emperor begins with a divine mandate from heaven; eventually his dynasty falls into corruption; and a new dynasty emerges with a new divine mandate. But the general pattern is still downward. Among modern Western historians, Arnold Toynbee is the one who developed this with most erudition, surveying over twenty ancient and modern civilizations. His conclusion was that there is a cyclical pattern in the history of civilization, and its overall direction is always downwards.

God will respond in mercy when his people confess their sins

Fourthly, however (and more optimistically), the pattern in Judges does encourage us to believe that God in his mercy will respond to the prayers of his people when they are willing to confess their sins. Furthermore, it suggests that frequently the way in which he will inject new hope after a period of distress is by raising up a leader.

There is a very strong doctrine of leadership in the book of Judges. In national history the leader may be a politician. Some of us would want to say perhaps that Winston Churchill was raised up in just such a fashion, in response to the prayers of people in this country. In church history it may be a great evangelist like John Wesley or George Whitefield who is used by God to turn the tide of spiritual declension and bring about revival. In the history of individual churches, too, it is not difficult to detect how the variations in the fortunes of a congregation are tied to the leadership which that church enjoys at any particular moment. It seems that God puts a lot more store by the contribution of the exceptional leader than Marx did.

No human deliverer ever meets our need

Finally, however, we see in this book of Judges that no human deliverer can ever fully meet our need. Although the judge appears and some temporary remission is granted on the downward spiral, it is only a temporary remission, never a total reversal of the pattern.

There is a very good reason for this. The judge always dies. Notice the emphasis that the narrator gives to that sad truth. So long as the judge is alive, everything gets better again; there is peace and security. But then he dies and it's back to square one. And the people have to wait decades upon the gracious providence of God before another judge brings security and peace once again. It is the recurring story that we find as we read the history of these judges.

Eventually, the people of Israel tried to escape their state of being hostage to death by appointing a dynastic monarch. One of the forces driving the period of judges in the direction of monarchy was the desire to escape the uncertainties that arise from a judge's finite lifetime. Once a dynastic monarchy is on the throne, when the king dies there is always a successor in line. But reading on in the books of Samuel and Kings shows us that this was no real solution either. There was no guarantee that the successor would be the kind of godly person whom the Spirit of God would be pleased to anoint and bless. So, in the later history of Israel, as often as not it is the kings who lead the people into idolatry.

The hard truth is that no human leader can really meet our needs. If they do nothing else wrong, they always eventually die.

But, by teaching the Israelites that pattern in history, God was preparing them for a leader yet to come, who would not die. In this book we are going to be looking at the stories of some fascinating characters: Gideon, Samson and Jephthah. None of them are perfect men, by a very long chalk. But each of them in his own way does prepare the ground for the true Judge and the true Saviour, Jesus.

II
People who
made history

1

Gideon:
an unexpected hero
Judges 6 – 8

The angel of the LORD came and sat down under the oak in Ophrah that belonged to Joash the Abiezrite, where his son Gideon was threshing wheat in a winepress to keep it from the Midianites. When the angel of the LORD appeared to Gideon, he said, 'The LORD is with you, mighty warrior.'

'But sir,' Gideon replied, 'if the LORD is with us, why has all this happened to us? Where are all his wonders that our fathers told us about when they said, "Did not the LORD bring us up out of Egypt?" But now the LORD has abandoned us and put us into the hand of Midian.'

The LORD turned to him and said, 'Go in the strength you have and save Israel out of Midian's hand. Am I not sending you?'

'But Lord,' Gideon asked, 'how can I save Israel? My clan is the weakest in Manasseh, and I am the least in my family.'

The LORD answered, 'I will be with you, and you will strike down all the Midianites together' (6:11–16).

How a hero is called and made

Are you one of those people who are easily frightened? Some quite simple things throw people into dread. I'm not very brave about the dentist, to be honest, whereas my wife is very nervous about wasps in the car. An over-crowded lift is enough to throw some people into claustrophobic terror. Most of us have a pet anxiety like this and some of us have several. Television announcers in my youth always used to warn you before a nasty play or film came on: 'Those of a nervous disposition may wish to turn their television off.'

Maybe you're the indecisive type? People like this are legion, too. They hesitate for ages and ages. I heard of a man who was engaged to a girl for ten years and still couldn't pluck up the courage to tie the nuptial knot. He just couldn't make up his mind.

These two personality traits quite often go together, don't they: nervousness and indecision? They are perhaps both manifestations of the same rather timid, insecure personality, and they tend to reinforce one another.

If you are that kind of person then Gideon is the man for you. For Gideon seems to have been that way too. He was indecisive and he was nervous. In fact, he was a wretched jumble of anxiety, inferiority and irresolution.

But his story tells us how out of this unpromising human material, God makes a hero. As we saw in the last chapter, so often the striking feature of the judges is that they are not the sort of people you would naturally assume to be leaders. So if there's hope for Gideon, there is hope for us, isn't there?

Let us trace the line of the story, and see what this man had to go through in order to become the hero that God made him.

Step One: A personal encounter with God

It all begins with this personal encounter with God, or the word of God. Did you notice how he is addressed in verse 12: 'The LORD is with you, mighty warrior'?

A few years ago the telephone rang one morning in my office and I was rather unnerved to hear a hushed voice saying, in tones of exaggerated solemnity, 'Good morning, Archbishop.' It was several seconds before I could collect myself sufficiently to reply. Then I discovered, of course, it was really a friend having a joke. But I suspect that the nonplussed feeling that I experienced when addressed in such unexpectedly lofty tones was not unlike Gideon's reaction to how the Lord introduces himself here. 'Mighty warrior?' Gideon must have thought. 'I'm no hero. The mere fact that I'm doing what I am doing proves that. What sort of idiot threshes his corn in a wine-press?'

Those of us who are used neither to wine-making nor threshing may not immediately see the incongruity here. The point is, corn is supposed to be threshed in an open place where the wind can blow the chaff away; but a winepress is a hollow in the rocks surrounded by walls, an altogether unsuitable place for threshing. Why is Gideon threshing corn in a winepress?

'Because I'm afraid,' Gideon would have to answer. 'The Midianites, a tribe of marauding raiders, are terrorizing the countryside hereabout. If I thresh the corn out in the open I'm sure they'll spot me and steal the harvest. So, coward that I am, I'm threshing it in here, in the cramped security of the winepress. "Mighty warrior", indeed! Anyone less like a mighty warrior would be hard to imagine. I'm the weakling of the family. Didn't you know that? I don't have a military background. You've got it all wrong, Lord. Look at me. I'm no soldier!'

But the angel of the Lord will not be deterred. 'Go in the strength you have and save Israel out of Midian's hand. Am I not sending you? ... I will be with you, and you will strike down all the Midianites together' (6:14, 16).

It is a very simple, obvious lesson, but nonetheless true: the first thing a person with a nervous or indecisive temperament like Gideon has to have, if they're going to achieve anything in the way of Christian service, is the conviction that God has personally and sovereignly intervened in their lives and called them to do something. Of course, you can exaggerate the importance of a sense of personal calling. But you can also grossly underestimate it. For most of us, a conviction that God has called us to do something is vital, if we're to have the courage to step out and do it. Otherwise we are afraid and insecure because we lack self-confidence. Our egos aren't strong enough to enable us to assert ourselves, to take initiatives, as mighty warriors must.

The interesting and I think exciting thing, however, is that the type of personality that we may call inadequate or self-effacing is precisely the sort of person whom God often chooses to do his work. Perhaps it is because as far as he is concerned, humility is a more important quality than ability. Perhaps it is because he can compensate for weakness very easily. Being omnipotent, God has a lot of strength at his disposal. What he cannot tolerate is pride.

Are you feeling demoralized? If so, be encouraged. Perhaps this is where your route back to self-respect begins, with Gideon. What is it that Paul writes? 'God chose the foolish things of the world to shame the wise; God chose the weak things of the world to shame the strong' (1 Corinthians 1:27). He has chosen the weak, lowly and despised – mere nothings, he says – to bring to naught people who think they are something, so that no-one can boast in his presence.

It is possible that our fears, our inadequacies and even our failures are, paradoxically, the very things that open us up to being useful to God. The arrogant think they can cope with their lives. If we think that, it could be the biggest barrier to our ever experiencing the kind of intervention in our lives that Gideon experienced. But once we admit our frustration with ourselves, once we're willing to confess our helplessness, God may well be there; and not to gloat over our lack of confidence, but to counteract it.

Do you see how he surrounds Gideon's fragile ego – so prone to defeatism and self-despair – with the impregnable wall of his own divine ego? Note the first-person singular pronouns. 'Go in the strength you have,' he says. '*I* am sending you, *I* am with you, *I* am the one who calls you, mighty warrior.'

Step Two: A stand within his family

Before he 'goes public' God puts Gideon through a kind of 'trial run'. Gideon's first task is a personal stand of testimony among his own family and close neighbours.

> That same night the LORD said to [Gideon], 'Take the second bull from your father's herd, the one seven years old. Tear down your father's altar to Baal and cut down the Asherah pole beside it. Then build a proper kind of altar to the LORD your God on the top of this height' (6:25–26).

This is unexpected!

Gideon's father, Joash, was an idolater. Like many Jews in this period of the judges, despite his background in biblical religion he had allowed his contact with pagan culture to compromise him. His old faith in Jehovah had slipped away. And the more sensual worship of the fertility gods of Canaan – Baal and Asherah – had taken its place.

Of course the same has happened in our society. A few centuries ago the Christian faith was a living religion for a very large proportion of our people, but with the passage of the years and the assault of materialism and humanism upon us, the spirituality of many in our country has declined. They worship the less demanding gods of twentieth-century affluence. They may still nominally call themselves Christians, but in practical terms the God of the Bible has very little place in their lives. It was like that for Joash. And it seems that the first step in Gideon's deliverance from his paralysing fears and indecision was to put that right. If he could not learn to take the lead in bringing his own family out of paganism, how would he ever lead the nation that way?

The author surely intends a lesson for us here. Many Christians are rather like lighthouses. Their witness streams afar, but the area around their home base is plunged in darkness. Of course it is very difficult to make a stand for Christ within your own family, particularly whenliving with your parents. But we will never develop into mighty warriors, I suspect, if we cannot find the necessary courage to do so. Gideon found it, to his credit, though not without his nervous temperament showing through.

> So Gideon took ten of his servants [notice, he wasn't going to do it on his own] and did as the LORD told him. But because he was afraid of his family and the men of the town, he did it at night rather than in the daytime (6:27).

Gideon was the sort of person who, if he thought he ought to speak to someone about Christ, would send them a gospel tract anonymously through the post. But at least it was a start; albeit with ten people to make sure he felt secure, and in the dark rather than in the daytime. Notice the effect it had on his father:

> The men of the town demanded of Joash, 'Bring out your son. He must die, because he has broken down Baal's altar and cut down the Asherah pole beside it.'
> But Joash replied to the hostile crowd around him, 'Are you going to plead Baal's cause? Are you trying to save him? Whoever fights for him shall be put to death by morning! If Baal really is a god, he can

defend himself when someone breaks down his altar'
(6:30–31).

So it seems that Gideon's demonstration of opposition to his family's idolatry (clandestine though that demonstration was) may have had some effect on his father, perhaps even initiating a process of spiritual rehabilitation. Joash reasoned that if a god is so unable to defend himself as Baal seemed to be, was such a god really worth worshipping?

There is a story told of John Knox, the Scottish Protestant reformer, who was extremely hostile to the veneration and worship of images by the Roman Catholic church. It tells how he saw a wooden effigy of the virgin Mary and threw it into the sea, saying, 'She's light enough; let the Madonna learn to swim.' It was very lacking in tact and respect, and I apologize to any reader who may find it offensive. But it very effectively illustrates the futility of venerating lifeless objects. Joash seems to reason similarly; though he didn't have the moral and spiritual strength to break free of his bondage to superstition on his own, there is a sneaking regard, perhaps even gratitude, towards his son for having done so. And in our own families the same will sometimes be true.

As fathers we may be older than our sons, but we're not necessarily wiser. We may have experienced more of life, but it is conceivable they have experienced more of God. So take a lesson from Joash. Have the grace to profit from your children's rebuke. More than one father has been embarrassed by his son's youthful spiritual zeal, yet turns out to be proud of him in later years. I suspect Joash may have been one of them.

43

Step Three: A special gift from God

> Now all the Midianites, Amalekites and other eastern
> peoples joined forces and crossed over the Jordan and
> camped in the Valley of Jezreel. Then the Spirit of the
> LORD came upon Gideon, and he blew a trumpet,
> summoning the Abiezrites to follow him. He sent
> messengers throughout Manasseh, calling them to
> arms, and also into Asher, Zebulun and Naphtali, so
> that they too went up to meet them (6:33–35).

What was the secret of the great heroes of the Bible? What
made them great people for God? Was it their natural
abilities and genius? Was it their training? Was it the consequence of the particular circumstances in which they
happened to find themselves? All these contribute up to a
point. But there were many other people, I guess, equally
gifted, equally well prepared, who were not used in the
signal way they were.

The real clue lies in God's choosing to equip these
people in a special way. We see it again and again. He
gives them a special job at a special moment in history,
but he equips them in a special way to do that job.

A major emergency has arisen here. A military danger
has escalated into a serious security threat. Israel stands
opposed to the joint assault of an alliance of Canaanite
tribes. The invasion, it seems, has already begun; the
enemy forces have crossed the River Jordan. The scattered
Israelite tribes seem helpless before the onslaught.
Without centralized military organization there seems
nobody capable of unifying them in the defence of their
territory; a major rout seems inevitable. Then out of
nowhere Gideon, this shy, ineffectual, timid little man

from Manasseh, suddenly emerges as a dynamic leader of men. He blows the trumpet summoning the tribal muster, mobilizing the national guard, as we would say, not only from his own local area but also from the neighbouring Israelite tribes of Asher and Zebulun and Naphtali. Within days he has an army of 32,000 men at his disposal.

How on earth did Gideon do it? Our narrator tells us, 'The Spirit of the LORD was upon Gideon.' The leadership charisma that he demonstrated, we're told, is not a natural gift. He didn't learn it at some military academy. He certainly didn't have it programmed into his genes. It was a supernatural endowment. The Spirit of the Lord came upon him. And we cannot run away from the truth that it is that same Spirit who endows us for leadership tasks today. Without him we will be powerless. 'But you will receive power when the Holy Spirit comes on you; and you will be my witnesses in Jerusalem, and in all Judea and Samaria, and to the ends of the earth' (Acts 1:8).' That was Jesus' promise.

Some of you may be confronting major challenges in your lives: new tasks, new callings. Maybe you feel that you are being summoned to exercise a role that does not come naturally to you and requires abilities and courage which you do not possess. If so, remember Gideon, the mighty warrior. We may be mighty warriors too, if the Spirit of God comes upon us. We must not be shy to ask for him, nor to act in his power when he comes.

Step Four: A special assurance from God

Gideon said to God, 'If you will save Israel by my hand as you have promised – look, I will place a wool

45

fleece on the threshing-floor. If there is dew only on the fleece and all the ground is dry, then I will know that you will save Israel by my hand, as you said.' And that is what happened. Gideon rose early the next day; he squeezed the fleece and wrung out the dew – a bowlful of water.

Then Gideon said to God, 'Do not be angry with me. Let me make just one more request. Allow me one more test with the fleece. This time make the fleece dry and the ground covered with dew.' That night God did so. Only the fleece was dry; all the ground was covered with dew (6:36–40).

Gideon was a man of indecisiveness and timidity, and the fact that the Spirit of God had filled him didn't change that natural temperament. It is very important to recognize that. Some people who are emotionally vulnerable feel cheated when they become Christians and don't overnight find their vulnerability disappearing. They still perhaps suffer from depression, anxiety or whatever it may be.

The reason is that the Holy Spirit doesn't erase our personalities and our old behaviour patterns in that way. He is an additional resource, not a substitute character or a ready-made new personality. In the gift of the Spirit, Gideon found the impulse, the fire in his belly, that he needed to blow the trumpet for God, but it's clear that he was still assailed privately by many doubts and much uncertainty. He needed not only power, but confidence. And the story of the fleece, perhaps the most famous aspect of the story of Gideon, has to do with how God gave him that confidence.

Some would like to inflate this incident into a regular

technique for obtaining Christian guidance. 'Whenever you are uncertain,' they say, 'put out a fleece. Ask God to do something miraculous to prove to you his will.' But that would be a very hazardous conclusion to draw, for the following reasons.

Firstly, *this is a one-off event.* You must always be careful about extrapolating from particular incidents into general principles. The line of biblical logic must always be the other way round. Learn your general principles and then interpret particular incidents in their light. This is a one-off event, and we do not, generally speaking, find men and women in the Bible being guided by this kind of somewhat bizarre experiment.

Secondly, *this is an Old Testament event.* It happens in the days before Pentecost. In those days we do find God guiding men and women occasionally by means of lots, and this is not a dissimilar means of guidance. But we never find the apostles in the New Testament advocating the lottery as a *normal* mode of Christian guidance. On the contrary, Paul prays that God would fill the Christians with the knowledge of his will 'through spiritual wisdom and understanding'. That's his ideal mode of guidance. That strongly suggests that, with the coming of the Holy Spirit upon all God's people in the New Testament, the need for lots and the like has disappeared.

Thirdly, *this is an event associated with a very major decision* – not only in Gideon's life, but in Israel's history. Huge issues hung upon the battle Gideon was to fight. The very existence of the Old Testament people of God was in jeopardy. In circumstances like that, we may perhaps anticipate that God would guide his servants in a direct and unmistakable fashion. It does not follow at all that he will agree to guide us in the same manner over

47

trivial issues. We must get a sense of proportion about how big an event this was, not just for Gideon, but for the history of Israel.

Fourthly, *this is an event in which the supernatural element is relatively unimportant.* For all we know, it might not have been supernatural at all. There may be a perfectly good scientific explanation for the preferential condensation of water vapour on surfaces under different physical conditions. Certainly no passer-by spotting Gideon's soggy fleece would have immediately detected the finger of God, as Moses did at the burning bush. He would simply have thought it was a rather odd thing and left it at that. You see, what Gideon was seeking was a special divine providence rather than a mind-blowing miracle. There is no encouragement in this story to think that God will look favourably upon those who requisition pillars of fire to order.

But the most important thing to observe about this incident is this: *Gideon's fleece was not a way of finding God's will at all.* If you read the story carefully you will see that Gideon already knew God's will. 'If you will save Israel by my hand as you have promised' – he gives himself away in the first sentence. God has already promised. What is significant is that 'if – '*If* you really mean it, God ...'

It was reassurance that this man was seeking, not guidance. If the fleece had been dry, it would not have meant that God did not intend to deliver Israel. He had already promised that he was going to. It would simply have meant that he refused to bolster Gideon's faith in that particular way. God was not answering his ignorance, he was answering his lack of confidence. In other words he was taking into account the timorous, indecisive element in Gideon's personality and he was graciously accommodating himself to it.

That is the real lesson to draw from Gideon's fleece. Not, 'Oh what a good technique for finding God's will!', but rather, 'What a wonderful example of God's patience and understanding attitude toward our natural fears and doubts.' There is nothing here to suggest that God is going to work miracles on demand for us; nothing to suggest that as Christians, we should spend all day looking for signs in the everyday things that happen to us. But if we are confronting a major crisis, if God really is calling us to take some major step of faith, and if by temperament we tend to be perhaps rather cautious, fainthearted, apprehensive people – then perhaps there is encouragement here to believe that God will find a way, through his special providences, to reassure us of his purpose. Something will happen; it will be insignificant to others perhaps, but meaningful to us, and it will give us the confidence we need to step out in faith, as we know deep down we should. Indeed, if the issue really is an important one, and if our heart really is anxious about it, perhaps there is encouragement here to ask God for such a special providence, for he is very understanding towards the fainthearted.

But if you do, let me remind you of the cautions implied here. Let the issue be a very important one. Let your fleece be a modest one. Let your purpose be to confirm guidance already received. Do not make the fleece the deciding factor. Finally, let your attitude to God in the whole exercise be wary of presumption, because we have no right to fleeces. If we start thinking that we do, we can be sure God will refuse to grant them. There is something rather endearing about the way Gideon says,

'Don't be angry with me.' As if to say, 'I know I'm really stepping over the mark here, God. I have no title to what I'm asking you for. Please, just be understanding to how fragile I'm feeling at this moment.'

So Gideon won the victory over his doubts. He discovered the confidence that he needed to obey God's call. And he stepped out.

And that brings us to the central, pinnacle point in his story.

Step Five: Practical faith

> The LORD said to Gideon, 'You have too many men for me to deliver Midian into their hands. In order that Israel may not boast against me that her own strength has saved her, announce now to the people, "Anyone who trembles with fear may turn back and leave Mount Gilead."' So twenty-two thousand men left (7:2–3).

There is a philosophy around these days: 'Bigger means better.' It's infiltrated the church more than a little. We're told that if we really want to be effective, if we really want to make an impact on the world, the things we do have to be big. Our budgets must be big, our public meetings must be big, our advertising must be big; the bigger the better.

I find a warning in Gideon's story against that kind of attitude. In fact, I find it in many places in the Bible. The trouble with bigness is that it so easily lulls us into a dangerous self-reliance. We become so self-inflated. I can imagine little Gideon, with the 32,000 men who had turned out for him, thinking, 'What a relief!' True, the allied forces of the enemies (according to 8:10) outnumbered him by four times. But nevertheless it gave Israel a fighting chance.

Ironically, that's exactly what God didn't want Israel to have. This seems to be the difference between human strategy and God's. We're concerned that our side should win. God, on the other hand, never has the slightest doubt on that score. He knows he can win. What matters to him is what the moral and spiritual consequences of victory will be in our lives. If winning is going to mean a lot of self-glorifying pride and complacency, then frankly, God would rather we lost. The only sort of victory he is interested in is one that draws his people closer to him and teaches them to depend on him. Hence the extraordinary advice to Gideon in chapter 7.

'Nice army you've got there, old chap! But unfortunately, with this many people, you could probably win without me. So if you want my help, you've got to get rid of a few.'

'Get rid of a few?' stammers Gideon, who has just winded himself blowing his trumpet up and down the countryside to muster all these forces. 'How many?'

'Oh, about 99% ... You can start by sending home everybody who's afraid. No, not you, Gideon; we've settled that, remember! You're staying. But everybody else who's afraid can have an honourable discharge. Now – how many have you got left? Ten thousand? Oh dear, far too even a match. It makes the odds only 30 : 1 against you. Far too good for any army of mine. We'll have to have a more rigorous selection procedure. Watch how they drink.'

'*Drink?*'

'Yes. Some will cup the water to their mouths, others

will bend right over and lap it with their tongues. Choose the former. Send the rest back as medically unfit, or something.'

Commentators have strained their brains to find some logic in this method of selection. Some suggest that people who cup the water to their mouths are more alert; they are keeping an eye out for the enemy. But I think that such rationalizations completely miss the point. The selection process is completely arbitrary. It is merely a way of whittling the numbers down. There is neither rhyme nor reason to it, humanly speaking.

So Gideon's vast army is reduced to a battalion of 300, and it is with this unlikely commando corps that Gideon routs the entire Midianite army. If you went to Sunday School you are familiar with the story. I've always thought that the novelist Alistair Maclean could have used it as the basis of a very good thriller. It makes *The Eagle Has Landed* look like a Sunday School picnic, what with its daring reconnaissance missions and cunning bluffs to outwit the enemy.

But the most characteristic feature of this battle was the war cry that the army was to shout. 'A sword for the LORD and for Gideon!' For this wasn't Israel's victory, it was God's, and Gideon wanted every one of his soldiers to know it. Oliver Cromwell likened his New Model Army to Gideon's. '300 good men and true with fear of God in them', he said, 'is better than 10,000 swept together by chance conscription or picked up for a shilling a head in the public house.' That is true, of course. Not only because they fight more bravely, or that they obey orders more promptly; but because God is pleased to vindicate such a company, no matter how small, because its only hope for victory in the conflict lies in him. He will not have us boasting that we have saved ourselves by our own strength. But his delight is to have his people celebrating victories won against all human odds because he has been their deliverer.

That's what the book of Judges is really all about. These judges are not heroes in the conventional sense. They are people who, in the power of God, deliver people in the name of God; and who give God the glory at the end of the story.

Applying Gideon's story to us

I am sure that your imagination is as capable as mine of seeking out the parallels that might rightly apply between Gideon's story and our own time.

We too have a fight to undertake, against the idolatries of our age, against the powers of evil that threaten the church in our day; the battle for truth and righteousness amidst error and sin. Some Christians have tried in the past to win that battle by the sword. That was a mistake, for ours is a battle against spiritual hosts of wickedness, and the New Testament makes it quite clear that the church differs from Israel of old in that it wields spiritual weapons, not worldly ones. But having understood that, the lesson of Gideon's victory is the lesson for us too. Humble, frightened and inadequate people like you and me may yet hope to be mighty warriors. Perhaps the pathway to that identity will be, for some of us, rather like Gideon's.

- A sense of personal calling; God does have a special job for us to do.
- An early testing of that calling; a courageous stand

among members of our own family perhaps.

- ► An equipping; clothed, against all the natural inabil-ities of which we are so conscious, with a power that we cannot explain other than to say that the Spirit of the Lord has gifted us.
- ► A special assurance; he is with us in this battle we're going to fight, so we need have no doubts about the outcome, which might weaken our resolve at the crucial moment.
- ► Practical faith; a faith that shows itself in not requir-ing huge numbers on our side in order to launch into the battle, but that is satisfied with a tiny handful of supporters whom we know that God has given us.

How Gideon refused the crown

So the victory was won. Gideon pursued the Midianite army until he had captured the two kings and personally executed them.

Now comes the unexpected twist to the end of the story, the part they always leave out in the Sunday School lessons. 'The Israelites said to Gideon, "Rule over us – you, your son and your grandson – because you have saved us out of the hand of Midian"' (8:22).

There was nothing unconstitutional about hereditary monarchy in Israel. Moses had made provision for it in the Law; it is there in the book of Deuteronomy. But strange to say, in this turbulent period of the judges it is often those who are the most committed to the religion of Moses who are the most suspicious about popular demands for a king. I think the reason is quite simple. Israel was unique: she had a covenant with God. Her laws, her victories, her government, all came from heaven. Such leaders as she had, whatever their title, had to be God-appointed not man-elected.

But it is clear that the Israelites who were offering the throne to Gideon were growing impatient with that political philosophy. In times of international crisis, it was altogether too hit-and-miss to wait around for God to raise up leaders when he felt like it. The nation needed to have a permanent commander-in-chief, and a reliable means of determining who would succeed him in office. Neighbouring pagan nations (notably, the Philistines) had solved this very problem by adopting dynastic monarchy as their political system. Why not Israel, too? 'Rule over us,' they said. 'You, your son and your grandson. Create a dynasty, Gideon.' But the motivation behind these monarchist aspirations was all wrong. It reflected a desire to move away from the theocratic ideals of the Israelite constitution towards a greater dependence on human government.

To give credit where credit is due, modest Gideon does seem, to some degree at least, to have detected this and repudiated it for the faithlessness it represented. 'I will not rule over you, nor will my son rule over you. The LORD will rule over you' (8:23). If only Gideon had stopped there! Then all the Sunday School stories would have been right. He would have gone down in history untarnished by any hint of shame. He would have been not only a great soldier, but also a great saint. If only that self-effacing humility that we saw in him at the very beginning, when he was threshing his corn in the winepress, had continued to characterize him to the end!

But sadly, it didn't. Gideon had changed. The shy stripling from an insignificant family in Manasseh had

55

been propelled into a national hero. He had become a success, and success had spoiled him. See how verse 24 goes on: '"I do have one request, that each of you give me an ear-ring from your share of the plunder." (It was the custom of the Ishmaelites to wear gold ear-rings.)' Was that so great a sin? After all, he'd won a great battle. Surely he deserved some financial reward out of all that booty he had taken? Well, perhaps. But there is something suspect, something rather grasping and unattractive about men who enrich themselves in such an opportunist manner.

And there was certainly something suspicious about what Gideon chose to do with the proceeds. 'Gideon made the gold into an ephod, which he placed in Ophrah, his town. All Israel prostituted themselves by worshipping it there, and it became a snare to Gideon and his family' (8:27).

'Ephod' is the word Moses had used to describe the richly decorated surplice that was made for the high priest to wear when he entered the sanctuary. But clearly what Gideon had made was not an ecclesiastical vestment but some kind of solid gold object. Most probably it was called an 'ephod', because, like the high priest's garment, it was a means of divination. It returned a yes or no answer when questions of personal guidance were put to it.

Poor Gideon had always had a problem with guidance and reassurance, you recall. No doubt he regarded his ephod as an excellent investment; a sort of permanent fleece, to have on tap whenever needed. Unfortunately, the guidance the ephod gave him and his compatriots was disastrous. Gideon led the people straight back into the kind of idolatrous mindset against which, at the beginning of his public career, he had so firmly stood.

Some commentators are disposed to be charitable towards Gideon's blunder over this ephod, regarding it as a well-meant gesture that turned out badly. 'He reserved some of the plunder to turn it into a memorial. It was a genuine attempt to set up a reminder of a great victory for the benefit of future generations. He couldn't possibly have intended to create an idolatrous cult by doing so.' On this argument, so far as Gideon was concerned, the ephod was merely a monument for the glory of Jehovah; it was the pagan inclinations of the people that turned it into an object of worship. They had done just that with the brass serpent Moses made in the wilderness. So Gideon ought not to be personally blamed.

Other commentators are more cynical. 'No. Gideon is not the angel that our Sunday School teachers described. That display of refusing the kingship? Mere diplomatic rhetoric. Political expediency, not theological conscience, made Gideon say no to the crown. The truth is, he was determined to establish his family as the centre of power in the country. The ephod was a clever move in that direction, for you notice he sets it up at Ophrah, his own family seat, so that all Israel has to come to his family seat to make use of it. Gideon had created a centralized shrine, and such shrines in the ancient world were always a focus for political as well as spiritual allegiance in a nation.' According to this view the story is a tragedy. Gideon was trying to turn Ophrah into a capital city, not unlike David's later centralization of the nation of Israel around Jerusalem when he brought the ark of the covenant to the city.

The truth, I would guess, probably lies between the two. The biblical historian does not seem to suggest any insincerity in Gideon's rejection of the monarchy, but on the other hand he does quite explicitly implicate Gideon himself in the ephod cult: 'All Israel prostituted themselves by worshipping it there, and it became a snare to Gideon and his family' (8:27). What's more, the narrator goes on to record some other suspicious elements in the closing description of Gideon's life, albeit without comment. In 8:30, for instance, he tells us Gideon had 'many wives'. A harem in those days was considered to be a royal prerogative. That does tend to suggest that Gideon did aspire to kingly office, *de facto* if not in theory. In 9:2 we read that seventy of Gideon's sons ruled over at least part of Israel's territory, which looks for all the world as if some kind of dynastic succession had been established, with or without a coronation. And is the name of Gideon's son in 8:31 significant? He was called Abimelech, which is the Hebrew for 'My father is king'.

It would be nice to do a whitewash job on Gideon's latter years. But there is no getting away from the facts. Gideon had changed. This self-effacing, humble young farmer of Manasseh had big ideas now. Success had gone to his head. It had spoiled him. And the result was that, as so often happens in this book of Judges, he left Israel no better than he found her; corrupted with idolatry, the seeds of which, ironically, he himself had sown.

Does not this aspect of the story beg for application? Especially, perhaps, to those of us who have made it in life, who have (in Disraeli's words) climbed to the top of the greasy pole. We need to beware the temptation that success brings. I've been in Cambridge now for nearly twenty years. I have watched a great many high-calibre young men and women pass through the university, and through my church, and I have seen the story again and again. Initially they demonstrate great promise and spiritual zeal as Christians. But when you come across them five or ten years later, you find that though they have achieved great success in their chosen careers they have gone off the boil spiritually. Sometimes they have ended in total spiritual shipwreck.

The golden ephods of today are all around us. Obelisks to achievement – we call them status symbols these days. They are snares to us and to our children. 'Nothing succeeds like success,' someone has said. Perhaps they should have said, 'Nothing fails like success.' For as the book of Proverbs reminds us, pride comes before destruction and a haughty spirit before a fall.

Of course, it may be God's will that we should be a great success. There may well be things that God is calling us to do in life for which we will gain great personal acclaim. And there may be nothing essentially wrong in that. But be sure of this: it will be a hundred times more difficult to sustain your spirituality at the top of the tree than it was at the bottom. As Gideon discovered.

2

The shadow of the past
Judges 9 – 12

Sometimes the past can cast a very long shadow. We make a mistake and we spend the rest of our lives reaping its consequences. Sometimes those consequences continue down the years even long after we're dead. The Ten Commandments talk about God 'punishing the children for the sin of the fathers to the third and fourth generation' (Exodus 20:5). And who has not seen that principle at work?

The book of Judges tells us the stories of two men, each in different ways disadvantaged by birth. One was the underprivileged son of a concubine, the other the child of a prostitute. I imagine that neither enjoyed the benefits of a father's discipline or shared in their father's inheritance. What is interesting is that each of them responds to this early disadvantage in different ways. Both become successful, both get to the top. But the shadow from the past catches up with them. In one case it makes the man resentful and aggressive; in the other, it seems to have taught him lessons of wisdom and diplomacy. Yet both these stories have tragic endings. And in each case the tragedy is linked to that long shadow from the past.

Abimelech

Abimelech's story begins in Judges 9. To understand it, you must realize that Jerub-Baal is another name for Gideon, whose story we have just been considering.

> Abimelech son of Jerub-Baal went to his mother's brothers in Shechem and said to them and to all his mother's clan, 'Ask all the citizens of Shechem, "Which is better for you: to have all seventy of Jerub-Baal's sons rule over you, or just one man?" Remember, I am your flesh and blood' (9:1–2).

Gilbert and Sullivan's *Ruddigore* includes the lines

> If you wish in this world to advance
> Your merits you're bound to enhance.
> You must stir it and stump it and blow your own trumpet
> Or trust me, you haven't a chance.

That is very often the case today. We live in a very individualistic and competitive society. It's very hard to get anywhere if you do not push yourself. Well – Abimelech is a warning to us on that score. Carried too far, such self-assertion can be dangerous and self-defeating. For this is the story of a man who was destroyed not so much by success, as by the obsessive ambition to succeed.

He was Gideon's son, but there was little family like-ness. No timorousness or diffidence checked Abimelech's advance. His philosophy right from the beginning was, look after Number One and let everybody else look after themselves – 'Do others before they do you.' Perhaps it was his underprivileged birth that gave him this aggres-sive, self-assertive character. I suspect he carried a deep resentment about his disadvantaged origins. This was a man with a score to settle and a chip on his shoulder. Though he was Gideon's son, you see, he was not his heir. His mother had been Gideon's concubine. That is a cate-gory of relationship we don't have these days; the best comparison is probably with a common-law wife or a kept mistress. She had never formally left her own family in order to marry into Gideon's family. For some reason she preferred to retain her own family ties at Shechem. But according to family law in the Middle East at that time, that meant that legally the children she bore Gideon, though they were not illegitimate, could only inherit from their mother's estate. They had no claim as Gideon's heirs.

That is the point. Abimelech had no share in Gideon's personal fortune when he died, nor in his dynasty (which, as we saw in the last chapter, seems to have emerged after his death in his seventy sons, despite the fact that Gideon had foresworn the crown). No doubt those seventy half-brothers wasted few words in explaining to Abimelech that he had no part in their new power base in Israel. It's hardly surprising in such circumstances that Abimelech grew up nursing a measure of bitterness toward his father's side of the family.

Was it Gideon or Abimelech's mother who gave him

his name – 'My father is king' – I wonder? Maybe that seed of ambition in him began very early indeed; maybe it was his mother's ambition rather than his own. There was certainly a shadow from the past lying across his life.

The path to power

But nothing could really justify the unscrupulous ambitious conspiracy that he undertook, to undermine his half-brothers. Machiavelli would have been hard pressed to put into operation a more brazen plan for securing political power. Notice in chapter 9 the stages that it follows.

Stage 1: He went to his mother's clan and sowed seeds of revolution in Shechem. 'Which is better for you: to have all seventy of Jerub-Baal's sons rule over you, or just one man? Remember, I [unlike them] am your flesh and blood' (9:2). Seeds germinate quickly, with the anticipated result: 'When the brothers repeated all this to the citizens of Shechem, they were inclined to follow Abimelech, for they said, "He is our brother." They gave him seventy shekels of silver from the temple of Baal-Berith' (9:3–4). Armed with this pagan fighting fund, Abimelech put into operation the next stage in his barbarous plot.

Stage 2: He hired 'reckless adventurers, who became his followers. He went to his father's home in Ophrah and on one stone murdered his seventy brothers, the sons of Jerub-Baal' (verses 4–5). Such a blood massacre was outrageous, even by the lax moral standards of those days. It was a blatant case of what Macbeth calls 'vaulting ambition'. Impervious to pity or shame, he ruthlessly eliminated those who obstructed his path to power. So

Abimelech achieved the next stage of his intrigue.

Stage 3: 'Then all the citizens of Shechem and Beth Millo gathered beside the great tree at the pillar in Shechem to crown Abimelech king' (9:6). He'd made it. He was a success, an accomplished exponent of that principle by which countless hundreds of tyrants have clawed their way to power: the end justifies the means. But it doesn't, of course. And with a dramatic genius worthy of Shakespeare, our narrator leaves it to Jotham, the sole survivor, to challenge the consciences of those involved. 'When Jotham was told about this, he climbed up on the top of Mount Gerizim and shouted to them, "Listen to me, citizens of Shechem, so that God may listen to you"' (9:7).

The Israelites, like all Middle Eastern people, loved riddles. Jotham's in verses 8–9 is a kind of allegorical word-puzzle. Doubtless, when he started to recite it at Abimelech's coronation, the guests – who would surely have failed to recognize Jotham on his rocky pulpit – must have assumed that this surprise orator was all part of the entertainment. He had, they thought, no doubt been hired to deliver a eulogy composed in honour of their new king. Mount Gerizim was the hilltop designated by Moses for the issuing of such public blessings. But as the fable unfolds, the smiles of condescending good humour must have drained from their faces. For this was not a blessing at all, but a curse.

> One day the trees went out to anoint a king for themselves. They said to the olive tree, 'Be our king.'
>
> But the olive tree answered, 'Should I give up my oil, by which both gods and men are honoured, to hold sway over the trees?'

Next, the trees said to the fig-tree, 'Come and be our king.'

But the fig-tree replied, 'Should I give up my fruit, so good and sweet, to hold sway over the trees?'

Then the trees said to the vine, 'Come and be our king.'

But the vine answered, 'Should I give up my wine, which cheers both gods and men, to hold sway over the trees?'

Finally all the trees said to the thornbush, 'Come and be our king.'

The thornbush said to the trees, 'If you really want to anoint me king over you, come and take refuge in my shade; but if not, then let fire come out of the thornbush and consume the cedars of Lebanon!' (9:8–15).

It doesn't demand a particularly acute mind to understand this masterpiece of allegory. Jotham is saying that men of real quality do not aspire to titles of kingship. They have better and more productive things to do with their lives than to wish to go lording it over other people. On the other hand, inferior and unworthy men are only too keen to take up such royal office when it is offered to them. The trouble is that, being essentially worthless and ignoble in character, they lack the personal resources to fulfil the fine promises they make. They turn out to be destructive and tyrannical. They are like megalomaniac brambles pretending to be lofty cedars. 'Come and take refuge in my shade,' says the bramble. What a laugh! When has a bramble ever protected anybody or anything? The only thing a bramble can do is spread fire; fire that destroys those foolish enough to take refuge in it.

Jotham's curse

So what is Abimelech? A noble cedar, anointed lord of the forest? Or a miserable thornbush with delusions of grandeur? Jotham has just enough time, it seems, before Abimelech's mercenaries get to his mountain platform, to tell the gathered crowd his opinion on the matter.

> Now if you have acted honourably and in good faith when you made Abimelech king, and if you have been fair to Jerub-Baal and his family, and if you have treated him as he deserves – and to think that my father fought for you, risked his life to rescue you from the hand of Midian (but today you have revolted against my father's family, murdered his seventy sons on a single stone, and made Abimelech, the son of his slave girl, king over the citizens of Shechem because he is your brother) – if then you have acted honourably and in good faith towards Jerub-Baal and his family today, may Abimelech be your joy, and may you be his, too! But if you have not, let fire come out from Abimelech and consume you, citizens of Shechem and Beth Millo, and let fire come out from you, citizens of Shechem and Beth Millo and consume Abimelech! (9:16–20).

So the curse was issued. And, says the sacred historian, in the course of time the curse came true.

> After Abimelech had governed Israel for three years, God sent an evil spirit between Abimelech and the citizens of Shechem, who acted treacherously against Abimelech. God did this in order that the crime

against Jerub-Baal's seventy sons, the shedding of their blood, might be avenged on their brother Abimelech and on the citizens of Shechem, who had helped him murder his brothers (9:22–24).

You can read in the rest of chapter 9 the gory details of the mutual slaughter that ensued. By the end, both the population of Shechem and Abimelech their king lay dead. As so often in these Old Testament books, the inspired historian is content to let history speak for itself.

> Thus God repaid the wickedness that Abimelech had done to his father by murdering his seventy brothers. God also made the men of Shechem pay for all their wickedness. The curse of Jotham son of Jerub-Baal came on them (9:56–57).

Notice, 'God repaid', 'God made'. Look back to verse 23: 'God sent an evil spirit.' Verse 24: 'God did this in order that ...' According to our historian, it is not chance that breaks this unholy alliance, with such bloody consequences. It is divine judgment, working through human affairs. That, of course, is what the Machiavellian conspirators of Abimelech's stamp never reckon on. We live in a moral universe. There is a God in heaven who hears the cry of innocent blood and avenges it. And as often as not, there is an ironic edge to the way that he avenges it. In this case it is the falling out of the two conspirators, Abimelech and Shechem, that results eventually in their mutual destruction.

There is a lesson here in the story of Abimelech, then, not so much for those who have achieved success as for those who aspire to it. Our methods *do* matter. The end does *not* justify the means. In God's world it is means that determines ends every time. As the apostle Paul puts it, whatever a man sows, that shall he also reap. Or as our Master put it, even more candidly, those who live by the sword shall die by the sword.

Whether we work in business or in churches, we need to take note of the salutary warning of Abimelech. No doubt we all want to succeed. But beware of too reckless an ambition! In particular, beware of an ambition that overrules your moral judgment concerning the methods you are prepared to use to obtain what you want.

Into the mouth of the dying Cardinal Wolsey, Shakespeare puts these words in his play *Henry VIII*.

> Cromwell, I charge thee, fling away ambition:
> By that sin fell the angels; how can man then,
> The image of his Maker, hope to win by it?
> Love thyself last: cherish those hearts that hate thee;
> Corruption wins not more than honesty.
> Still in thy right hand carry gentle peace,
> To silence envious tongues. Be just, and fear not:
> Let all the ends thou aim'st at be thy country's,
> Thy God's, and truth's; then, if thou fall'st,
>   O Cromwell,
> Thou fall'st a blessed martyr! (III ii)

It sounds, perhaps, a little like the moralizing of a public school headmaster, but it is true; it is more important how you win, than whether you win. Learn from Abimelech's disaster how destructive success can be when bought at the price of a good conscience.

Learn too the perils that lurk in unresolved shadows from the past. Abimelech was a man with a chip on his shoulder. That disadvantage of his birth had been allowed to breed bitterness and resentment in his soul. And it fatally clouded his judgment. Shadows from the past have a way of doing that.

Jephthah's story

> Jephthah the Gileadite was a mighty warrior. His father was Gilead; his mother was a prostitute (11:1).

Aldous Huxley makes an interesting comment about success in his book, *Proper Studies*. Referring to a term coined by psychologist William James, he says, 'Success is the bitch goddess. She demands strange sacrifices from those who worship her.'

That could almost be an epitaph to Jephthah. Of all the men in the Bible, I find his story one of the most movingly tragic. For here is a good man, very different from Abimelech. This is not some ruthless, driven person; it is not the temptation of success that gets to Jephthah. It is not unscrupulous vaulting ambition to succeed that ruins him. And yet success, bitch-goddess that she is, still contrives to damage him. She does not spoil him or destroy him, she simply conspires to break his heart. 'A strange sacrifice' just about sums up Jephthah's personal tragedy.

The circumstances of his birth placed Jephthah in a much worse social situation than that of Abimelech. For Jephthah was the child of a prostitute, which meant that he had no legal rights within his maternal family at all. When his half-brothers turned on him, there was nowhere to go but into the criminal underworld. That is where he went, and that is where he thrived. For though he had no inheritance, he did have a charismatic gift of leadership, and also, perhaps, a good pair of fists.

Gilead's wife also bore him sons, and when they were grown up, they drove Jephthah away. 'You are not going to get any inheritance in our family,' they said, 'because you are the son of another woman.' So Jephthah fled from his brothers and settled in the land of Tob, where a group of adventurers gathered around him and followed him (11:2–3).

Jephthah's rise to greatness

Left to himself, he would probably have continued happily playing Robin Hood with his gang of bandits for the rest of his life. No doubt, like Abimelech, he did have a chip on his shoulder about having been treated badly by his half-brothers, but unlike him he was not consumed with the lust for revenge.

On the contrary, Jephthah seems to have been quite a spiritual man. Underneath his outlaw macho image there is a very profound, if rather ill-taught, faith in God. We see the first sign of it when fortune takes a hand in his career. 'Some men are born great,' says Shakespeare, 'some achieve greatness, and some have greatness thrust upon them.' It was the last of those routes that prevailed for Jephthah.

Some time later, when the Ammonites made war on Israel, the elders of Gilead went to get Jephthah from the land of Tob. 'Come,' they said, 'be our commander, so we can fight the Ammonites' (11:4).

National emergencies have a way of bringing leaders to the fore. It would be quite wrong to portray Jephthah as an opportunist. It was his own clan leaders who summoned him back to take the helm, just as Charles de Gaulle was recalled in a later episode in European history. It must have been very humiliating for them to have to do it. Jephthah in his response couldn't resist rubbing salt in the wound, easing that chip on his shoulder a little and watching them squirm and grovel:

> Jephthah said to them, 'Didn't you hate me and drive me from my father's house? Why do you come to me now, when you're in trouble?'
> The elders of Gilead said to him, 'Nevertheless, we are turning to you now [*Grovel, grovel!*]; come with us to fight the Ammonites, and you will be our head over all who live in Gilead' (11:7–8).

Not as king, you notice. The Israelites seem to have learned that lesson, at least for a while. They are asking Jephthah to become a judge – a non-hereditary commander in chief, raised up to meet the exigencies of a military crisis. It is his reply to that offer that provides evidence that Jephthah had some sense of personal dependence on God:

> Jephthah answered, 'Suppose you take me back to fight the Ammonites and the LORD gives them to me – will I really be your head?'
> The elders of Gilead replied, 'The LORD is our witness; we will certainly do as you say.' So Jephthah went with the elders of Gilead, and the people made him head and commander over them. And he

71

repeated all his words before the LORD in Mizpah (11:9–11).

Paganism was rife in those days. So the fact that the name of Jehovah is given such prominence in this covenant between Jephthah and the elders of Gilead is very significant. He does not grasp at the reins of power. They are placed in his hands, not without some measure of reluctance and even suspicion on his part. Jephthah was not interested in any kind of office except one that was constitutionally ratified in a proper manner with the Lord at the heart of it. The same statesmanship and God-centred sensitivity emerges, I think, in the exchange he initiated with the Ammonites:

> Then Jephthah sent messengers to the Ammonite king with the question: 'What do you have against us that you have attacked our country?' (11:12).

Here's a man who does not shoot first and ask questions afterwards. Maybe his years of banditry in the desert had taught him to be wary of violence and use it only as a last resort. Certainly his reply to the king of Ammon's territorial demands is a model of international diplomacy: candid and yet tactful; firm, yet conciliatory. He yields no ground, yet he leaves the enemy an opportunity to withdraw without humiliation, which is a very important tactic in any political negotiations.

Notice, he points out that the land in question has never belonged to the Ammonites anyway. Israel acquired the territory by right of conquest from the Amorites – a quite different group of people, who were foolish enough to make a fight for it. They had been occupying it now for three centuries without any Ammonite protest. In international law there was no question but that the Ammonite demands were quite groundless. They should be satisfied with what they already had. 'Will you not take what your god Chemosh gives you? Likewise, whatever the LORD our God has given us, we will possess' (11:24). He is willing even to make a politically correct nod in the direction of theological pluralism: 'Let justice, not violence, prevail,' he advises, 'and let us respect our mutual religious traditions.'

> I have not wronged you, but you are doing me wrong by waging war against me. Let the LORD, the Judge, decide the dispute this day between the Israelites and the Ammonites (11:27).

It certainly wasn't Jephthah's fault that peace negotiations broke down. At the end of the day, however, he found himself faced with an implacable foe: 'The king of Ammon, however, paid no attention to the message Jephthah sent him' (11:28). This enemy was bent on invasion and war was therefore inevitable.

Those who wish to style themselves pacifists have never really grappled with the political reality of a situation like this. Sometimes very wicked people gain power in this world, and they will not settle for anything except a fight. Jephthah does not like war; he does his best to avoid it. But at the end of the day he is left with no alternative. So, just as Gideon did, he mobilizes his tribal forces; he musters the national guard. 'The Spirit of the LORD came upon Jephthah. He crossed Gilead and Manasseh, passed through Mizpah of Gilead, and from there he advanced against the Ammonites' (verse 29).

And it is then, right at this point of military crisis, when the adrenaline is pumping through Jephthah's veins, that success – that bitch-goddess – strikes her blow.

Jephthah's vow

> And Jephthah made a vow to the LORD: 'If you give the Ammonites into my hands, whatever comes out of the door of my house to meet me when I return in triumph from the Ammonites will be the LORD's, and I will sacrifice it as a burnt offering' (11:30).

Why on earth did he make such a foolish vow? Every action of this man up to now has seemed wise. Why does he suddenly descend to such a foolish, superstitious promise? Commentators have asked themselves that question over and over again.

This is another of those interesting episodes in the biblical narrative where the sacred historian leaves the interpretation of the story in the hands of the reader. He doesn't tell us why Jephthah made this vow. He just reports that he did. He leaves it to us, who are caught up in the characterization and the plot, to put ourselves into the story and imagine why. It is the characteristic of all good stories that they are 'open' to the reader's involvement in this way. We ought not to be shy of recognizing that this is the case in many Bible stories too.

The text, then, invites us to understand this man. What is going on inside him? He was not naturally given to gratuitous violence. He was not naturally given to pagan superstition. He was not naturally consumed by unscrupulous ambition. So far as we have seen he is a

God-fearing, good, wise man. But he really wanted to win that battle against the Ammonites! He had never wanted anything in his life more. He went to battle with an almost insane commitment. Because Jephthah, remember, for all his noble character, had a chip on his shoulder. He, too, was haunted by a shadow from the past. And this was his God-given chance to shed that burden. All his life he had nursed the grudge of what his clan had denied him; now at last he could salvage his wounded pride; now at last he could soothe those injured feelings. Now at last he could make them eat humble pie and admit the wrongs they had done him. All he had to do was win this battle, and the grievance of a lifetime would be propitiated. He would be their head. Boy, how he was going to enjoy that!

'Why,' he said to himself as he rode to meet the enemy, 'I'd give anything to win this battle, anything. Do you know that, God? I'd give *anything*.'

> Then Jephthah went over to fight the Ammonites, and the LORD gave them into his hands. He devastated twenty towns from Aroer to the vicinity of Minnith, as far as Abel Keramim. Thus Israel subdued Ammon. When Jephthah returned to his home in Mizpah, who should come out to meet him but his daughter, dancing to the sound of tambourines! She was an only child (11:32–34).

You don't have to be able to read the Hebrew to feel the pathos of this section of the narrative. Picture it in your mind's eye. Jephthah returning home; already, no doubt, the success of battle beginning to fade a little and doubts invading his mind, regret about that rash promise he had made; anxiety beginning to disturb him about whom it might implicate. Meanwhile, back at home, there's his daughter; a lively young teenager. She was an only child. It doesn't take much to imagine how devoted such a girl would have been to her father. No doubt he had told her many times, tucking her into bed at night, of how Miriam had greeted Moses after the defeat of Pharaoh with tambourine and dancing. She resolved that she would meet her dad the same way, as he came back from the great victory he had won for Israel.

And so the drama reaches its climax. 'When he saw her, he tore his clothes and cried, "Oh! My daughter! You have made me miserable and wretched, because I have made a vow to the LORD that I cannot break"' (11:35).

Some commentators have tried to soften the scandal of these verses by suggesting that Jephthah, when making his vow, had in mind some domestic animal. But that really won't hold water; the Hebrew clearly implies it was a human being he was offering to sacrifice. And that being so, there is no way to minimize the inexcusable folly of the vow.

It was inexcusable, firstly, of course, because of *its immoral contempt for the sanctity of human life*. Life may have been cheaper in those days, but Jephthah knew the fifth commandment. War is one thing, murder quite another.

It was inexcusable, secondly, because of *its pagan assumption that God can be manipulated by such barbaric gestures*. No doubt Jephthah was ill-taught, and as a result had not escaped the influence of Canaanite superstition; but he was familiar enough with the law of Moses to know that human sacrifice was explicitly forbidden in Israel, and utterly repugnant to the Lord.

And thirdly, it was inexcusable because of *Jephthah's*

proud refusal to accept responsibility for his mistake and revoke his vow. Do you see what he says in verse 35? 'My daughter! You have made me miserable and wretched ...' Isn't that just like a man? '*You* have made me miserable and wretched.' As if *she'd* done something wrong. How often do we try to transfer the blame on to others in just that way? The right course of action would have been to accept that he had made the most appalling blunder. The right course of action would have been to break his foolish promise and accept whatever judgment God might send as a penalty for that broken vow. He was the one responsible for this situation, not his daughter. There is always, you know, such a thing as the lesser of two evils, and Jephthah here conspicuously fails to recognize the fact.

> After the two months [that she requested], she returned to her father and he did to her as he had vowed. And she was a virgin. From this comes the Israelite custom that each year the young women of Israel go out for four days to commemorate the daughter of Jephthah the Gileadite (11:39–40).

Aldous Huxley was right. Success does demand strange sacrifices from those who worship her. Sometimes it demands the sacrifice of our children.

The lesson of Jephthah

The lesson we learn from the story of Jephthah is not that success can go to your head – that was Gideon's problem. It was not that ambition to succeed can sear the conscience – that was Abimelech's disaster. No: Jephthah is a figure of tragedy because in one single, blinding, head-strong moment of folly he wanted success more than he wanted anything else in the world. And success, bitch-goddess that she is, claimed her pound of flesh in that instant.

So here's a lesson to store up in your heart for those unexpected moments when the opportunity to make it suddenly descends upon you. This is a lesson for good men, self-controlled men, wise, spiritual men, family men. Never, never, never make success an idol, not even for an instant. And especially, never gamble your children for it. How many men are there, wringing their hands in quiet desperation and saying to themselves, 'Why did I do it? Why did I put my career before my marriage? Why did I put promotion before my children? Why did I put my so-called ministry before all those things that God gave me as priority to care for in my life?'

Learn from Jephthah. There are always more impor-tant things than success. Sometimes, in the heat and exhilaration of the chase, even the best of people forget that, to their cost. Of course, it was the shadow from the past that made him vulnerable. If it hadn't been for that grievance he nursed, if it hadn't been for that chip on his shoulder, if it hadn't been for that old score he needed to settle, that old weakness, that damage to his self-image that he needed so badly to repair – if it wasn't for that, he would have resisted the temptation, surely, of that silly, silly vow. Shadows from the past have a nasty way of dis-torting your judgment. Beware of them. They could cost you and your family dear.

3

Samson: a strong man's weakness
Judges 13 – 16

There is a hunger for heroes today.

We have plenty of celebrities, of course. But celebrities
are famous not for their achievements, but for the media
image they project. Real heroes are hard to find. In fact,
these days they are largely confined to the celluloid of the
movie film. Bruce Willis in *Die Hard*, Sylvester Stallone,
Jean-Claude Van Damme, and of course Mr Universe
himself, Arnold Schwarzenegger. They are all part of a
myth that goes back centuries. Some years ago there was
a TV cartoon series called '*He-man, Master of the
Universe*'. I remember it well, because my son insisted that
for Christmas he had to have a plastic model He-man. It
was absolutely necessary for his survival as a respectable
member of his peer group at school for him to have one
of these little dolls. So I visited Hamley's in London – 'the

largest toyshop in the world' — to try to buy one. I was told that such was the demand that they had run out of stock within hours of the toys being delivered.

Had Hamley's read their history books a little more carefully, maybe they wouldn't have been so unprepared for the doll's success. Muscle-bound warriors like He-man, the strongest man in the universe, appear as popular folk legends in just about every nation on earth. In fact, this cartoon represented a rather enterprising commercial synthesis of those ancient themes, a kind of blonde and youthful Odin fused with a brawny and athletic Hercules. He-man's extraordinary ability to excite the imagination of the young demonstrates just how deeply these heroic images are embedded into our cultural heritage.

Many commentators regard Samson as just one more example of the persistence of this type of epic champion in the world's fairy tales. He too is He-man, the strongest man in the universe. They point out that his tearing apart of a lion single-handed, and his uncongenial experience of forced labour in the darkness of enemy captivity, both have analogies with the stories of Hercules in Greek mythology. Some have even suggested that the name 'Samson', which probably derives from the Hebrew word for 'sun', indicates some kind of connection to the solar myths of other pagan Near-Eastern cultures.

I believe that the evidence for that is thin to the point of non-existence. But there is a sense in which scholars who want to identify some kind of more general 'sympathetic vibration' between these chapters in Judges and ancient mythology may be right. After all, mythology is not quite the same thing as fiction; romanticized, embroidered and exaggerated it may no doubt be, but at the root of all mythology lies not human invention, but human memory. Once upon a time giants did walk on earth; godlike in physique, titanic in their exploits. Once upon a time there was a heroic age, now lost but not forgotten. It survives in the fantasy world of the toy shop and in television cartoons. And Samson perhaps does represent one aspect of the Bible's witness to the authenticity of those dimly remembered human prodigies of the past, like Nimrod the mighty hunter, Goliath the colossus of Gath, those terrifying sons of Anak and the mysterious Nephilim.

Samson is not a myth. His life is set very firmly in the historical context of the twelfth century before Christ, when the Philistines began to settle the coastal plain that we now call the Gaza Strip. But although he isn't a myth, Samson is very much the kind of stuff of which myths are made. It is not hard to imagine how fathers would have told the stories of his breathtaking adventures over and over again to wide-eyed sons who refused to go to sleep until they had heard them one more time. Maybe they even made little dolls representing him, with which to re-enact in play the drama of his mighty deeds. For unlike Gideon, Abimelech and Jephthah, Samson was not a leader of men. He was neither a general nor a politician. He was an individualist hero in the classic mould, a lone wolf (or, more appropriately perhaps, a rogue elephant).

He conducts an extraordinary one-man campaign against the Philistine menace. He does so entirely single-handedly. He doesn't need to raise the tribal muster like Gideon and Jephthah did. For Samson is 'The Terminator'; Samson is He-man; Samson is godlike in physique, titanic in his exploits, the strongest man in the universe.

Or is he?

That's the paradoxical half-answered question that hovers around these chapters of Judges. The story of Samson, for all its fairy-tale elements, has a very serious side. As recorded in the book of Judges, it's not just a romantic fantasy but a very down-to-earth tragedy. Nobody had more potential for being mythologized into a Hercules figure than Samson had, yet the book of Judges resolutely declines to present Samson to us as He-man. He is presented instead as a *hu-man* who, in spite of his phenomenal and even supernatural endowments, is all too ordinary, vulnerable and weak. That is the uniqueness of biblical narrative. It never idealizes its heroes. It never elevates them into mythical demigods, it never succumbs to the Hollywood stereotype.

In fact, though the novel as a literary genre was not to be invented until many centuries later, our inspired author's candid observation and psychologically penetrating biographical record of Samson often approaches the genius of a great novelist. This is the story of a human being. It is not mere legend, adventure story or myth. The sacred historian has something to teach us in these chapters, and he communicates it to us as novelists do; not by mythological symbols nor even by direct moralizing, but by presenting to us this drama of a human character with whom we empathize, and allowing us, in the openness of the text, to draw our own conclusions about this man.

Let me suggest three conclusions that, from my own reading of the story, I think can be drawn.

Even the best start in life
can be wasted

A certain man of Zorah, named Manoah, from the
clan of the Danites, had a wife who was sterile and
remained childless. The angel of the LORD appeared
to her and said, 'You are sterile and childless, but you
are going to conceive and have a son' (13:2–3).

The modern tendency is to blame all one's mistakes upon
one's parents: 'I had a bad upbringing' or 'I get it from my
father's side of the family.' Some strands of modern
psychology display a decidedly deterministic inclination
in that respect, interpreting all behaviour in terms of
genetics or environmental conditioning in infancy.

Samson could hardly complain on that score. No
shadow of the past can really be said to haunt him. Unlike
Abimelech and Jephthah, he had a privileged beginning.
True, there is a hint that it was his mother who ruled the
roost in his family home; his father by contrast displays a
rather ineffectual and nervous temperament. When he
hears the news of the promised pregnancy, instead of getting out the champagne, Manoah falls on his knees in
consternation: 'Then Manoah prayed to the LORD: "O
Lord, I beg you, let the man of God you sent to us come
again to teach us how to bring up the boy who is to be
born"'(13:8).

He was not the first man who has come close to faint-
ing when the awful responsibility of fatherhood descends
upon his shoulders, of course. But Manoah is a rather
extreme example of the paternity-anxiety complex. When

83

his prayer is answered and he discovers that his prophetic visitor was none other than an angel, he is thrown into an even more violent state of panic. "'We are doomed to die!" he said to his wife. "We have seen God!'" (13:22). Manoah is not the kind who keeps his head when all around are losing theirs.

But his wife is of a very different stamp. 'His wife answered, "If the LORD had meant to kill us, he would not have accepted a burnt offering and grain offering from our hands, nor shown us all these things or now told us this"' (13:23). Clearly, here is a woman of much greater common sense than Manoah, and with much more personal confidence too. A woman who can take angelic visitations and supernatural pregnancies in her stride must surely have been able to cope with bringing up a child, even one so strange as Samson, without laying the foundation of an over-neurotic infantile personality.

Perhaps she did spoil this late and only child, as perhaps mothers in that situation are rather prone to do. We will see some evidence of that later. Nevertheless, Samson was lucky. He was favoured in his godly, caring and conscientious parents, and favoured in his supernaturally ordained conception. He is not plucked out of obscurity like Abimelech or Gideon or Jephthah. From birth he is set aside for something special.

> See to it that you drink no wine or other fermented drink and that you do not eat anything unclean, because you will conceive and give birth to a son. No razor may be used on his head, because the boy is to be a Nazirite, set apart to God from birth (13:4–5).

The origin of the Nazirite vow is lost in antiquity. Its

roots may well be outside Israelite culture altogether. But what we do know is that the law of Moses gave the Nazirite vow a formal definition and a more specifically God-centred orientation. You can read about it in Numbers 6:1–21. A Nazirite had to vow that he would not do three things: drink alcohol; touch dead bodies; or cut his hair. These three abstentions symbolized a ritual holiness not unlike that of a high priest. The difference was that anyone could voluntarily adopt a Nazirite vow, whether they came from a priestly family or not; so it was a way in which highly motivated people in the Old Testament could express their singular dedication to God.

A Nazirite vow was made for some special purpose. A need for guidance, perhaps, or for healing. Samson's had to do with the strength needed to resist the steady growth of Philistine influence within Israel's borders. But whereas Nazirite vows usually lasted for a few weeks, Samson's began *in utero* and continued throughout his life.

So I suppose this was, in the language of Old Testament ritual, a way of saying that this man's consecration to the special task of national deliverance was totally wedded to his personality. Samson was a man who from the very womb of his mother had one all-consuming vocation. Not for him the torment of having to choose a career! He was quite literally born to be a hero: 'The woman gave birth to a boy and named him Samson. He grew and the LORD blessed him, and the Spirit of the LORD began to stir him' (13:24). So on top of all these other advantages, he received the supreme endowment. The Spirit of God, perhaps in response to that silent prayer which his Nazirite vow was, began to move him and endowed him with such strength that he could rout entire armies single-handedly.

Chapters 14 and 15 are punctuated by little pictures of just how phenomenally strong Samson was. In 14:6, 'The Spirit of the LORD came upon him in power so that he tore the lion apart with his bare hands as he might have torn a young goat' – this, while he was still a child in his parents' home! In 14:19, 'The Spirit of the LORD came upon him in power', and he struck down thirty men. In 15:14, 'The Spirit of the LORD came upon him in power', and he struck down 1,000 men. Incredible? Well, we must remember that these were days when weapons were simple and all fighting ultimately depended on brute strength and stamina. Our author doesn't say that bullets couldn't have killed Samson, merely that he was, in terms of physical prowess, a prodigy. He had a superhuman gift.

Gifts can be given, but they can also be taken away. 'He awoke from his sleep and thought, "I'll go out as before and shake myself free." But he did not know that the LORD had left him' (16:20).

I once visited a lady who was obviously deeply worried about her son. He had been getting himself into all kinds of trouble, and at the time of my visit was about to be prosecuted by the police for a violent assault. His mother was heartbroken. She told me that she had done everything for him, that he had everything going for him. She told me about the school he'd been to. He'd sung in the church choir, he had even sometimes assisted the priest at the altar. 'What did I do wrong?' she asked me.

Sometimes children bring disaster upon themselves and their parents have done nothing wrong at all. It is important to hold that in tension with what we have already observed about shadows from the past. We must not think that all the mistakes and tragedies of our children are our doing. What better start in life could Samson have had, than the one he had? He had all the advantages: the blessings, the gifts – he even had the Lord on his side, right from the start. Compare that devout young Nazirite of Dan, growing up under the blessing of God's Spirit that we encounter back in chapter 13, with the broken, humiliated, blinded, shackled ruin of a man of whom we read in chapter 16.

> Can this be he,
> That heroic, that renowned,
> Irresistible Samson? whom unarmed
> No strength of man, or fiercest wild beast
> could withstand.

So John Milton expresses the tragic contrast in his great epic, *Samson Agonistes*. In that poem he portrays Manoah coming to visit his son in his Philistine jail at the end of his life. He puts into Manoah's mouth the sentiments of a thousand parents who, like him, suffer the bitterness of disappointed hopes about their precious offspring:

> I prayed for children, and thought barrenness
> In wedlock a reproach; I gained a son
> and such a son as all men hailed me happy;
> Who would be now a father in my stead?

Doubtless Manoah and his wife asked themselves what they did wrong too. But the unspoken lesson of the story of Samson, surely, is that this was a man who destroyed himself. Gifts and advantages aren't everything, you see. In spite of all his strength, Samson was a moral weakling. And that moral weakness was quite literally the ruin of him, in spite of all his early advantages.

There is a vital lesson for us to learn there. Some of us are privileged people; we have advantages. Perhaps, like Samson, we have advantages of birth. Maybe we have been born into wealthy families. Perhaps some of us, like him, have been dedicated to God from our earliest years; our Christian, believing parents have done everything they reasonably could to secure our spiritual growth and our personal happiness. But if, like Samson, we lack moral fibre, then no matter how much we receive by way of advantage of birth, we will bring ruin on ourselves in the end, just as surely as he did. And we'll have no-one to blame but ourselves.

Some of us are talented. Talented athletes, perhaps, like Samson. Perhaps we are talented in the intellectual sphere. In either case, we can do things other people can't. Talent creates openings in life; our name might go down to posterity because of our achievements. But if we, like Samson, surrender to moral weakness, then our special powers – God-given though they may be – will waste away as surely as his strength did. Just like Samson, we will become helpless victims of a grim and painful situation that we can't control.

Some of us have spiritual gifts; we have experienced the Holy Spirit endowing us in unusual ways for a ministry that God has specially entrusted to us, just as it was for Samson. But if like him we surrender to moral weakness, then, for all our spiritual gifts and endowments, we may yet perish.

Saul was numbered among the prophets – and Judas was numbered among the Twelve. Jesus said that many would come to him on the Last Day, speaking of prophecies they had made and miracles they had worked in his name. 'Then I will tell them plainly, "I never knew you.

Away from me, you evildoers!"' (Matthew 7:23).

Samson was a very privileged man. Learn from his ruin that gifts are not everything. Even the best start in life can be wasted.

The peril of an undisciplined sexual appetite

One word sums up Samson's general attitude to life: we see it in him again and again. 'Immaturity'. There is something about Samson that is redolent of a child who has never grown up. That is why I wonder whether his mother spoiled him. There is something infantile about his behaviour.

Firstly, his frequent *frivolity*. A puerile irresponsibility characterizes a disturbing amount of what Samson does. Secondly, his *vindictiveness*. A childish, but very vicious, spitefulness colours his response whenever he can't get his own way. And thirdly, and most conspicuously, his *sensuality*. Freudian psychologists talk about children going through the 'oral phase' when everything goes into the mouth; some people, they say, become stuck in that phase all their lives. Samson is a case in point. He seems to be psychologically arrested at a stage of habitual self-indulgence; no self-control, no self-denial, just an incessant demand for the immediate gratification of his appetites. He was, as I say, immature; and it's in his relationships with women that this most clearly appears.

The prostitute of Gaza

One day Samson went to Gaza, where he saw a prostitute. He went in to spend the night with her. The people of Gaza were told, 'Samson is here!' So they surrounded the place and lay in wait for him all night at the city gate. They made no move during the night, saying, 'At dawn we'll kill him.' But Samson lay there only until the middle of the night. Then he got up and took hold of the doors of the city gate, together with the two posts, and tore them loose, bar and all. He lifted them to his shoulders and carried them to the top of the hill that faces Hebron (16:1–3).

The narrator is surely deliberately abrupt in his style there. 'He saw her and he went to spend the night with her' is actually a translator's euphemism; the Hebrew text is considerably more blunt in its description of the sexual intercourse which took place.

Here is Samson in typical mood; quite unable to bridle his passions, searching for immediate satisfaction of his lust. It's very difficult to believe that this was an isolated incident. I suspect the reason this particular incident has been selected is because his frivolity also took a hand. While he's with the prostitute, the Philistines in the city plot to ambush him. His response has a certain John Cleese quality; he tears out the doors of the city gate together with the two posts, lifts them on to his shoulders and carries them to the top of the hill that faced Hebron. The narrator leaves us to imagine the residents of Gaza waking up the following morning and wondering where their city gates have gone, only to discover that by some miracle of levitation, they're sitting on top of a mountain 38 miles away! It's the rag-week stunt to end all rag-week stunts.

But – as is sometimes the case with undergraduate humour – Samson's sense of fun doesn't always remain within the bounds of common sense or good taste. Take, for example, the fiasco of his abortive wedding.

The woman of Timnah

> Samson went down to Timnah and saw there a young Philistine woman. When he returned, he said to his father and mother, 'I have seen a Philistine woman in Timnah; now get her for me as my wife' (14:1–2).

You can hear once again the greedy self-indulgence behind that peremptory demand. Parental advice counts little when Samson's hormones are buzzing. 'His father and mother replied, "Isn't there an acceptable woman among your relatives or among all our people? Must you go to the uncircumcised Philistines to get a wife?"' (14:3).

A marriage between a Philistine girl and an Israelite was bound to cause suspicion and disapproval on all sides, especially when the man in question had a reputation like Samson's. We are told in 14:11 that when Samson laid on the traditional marriage feast, his Philistine in-laws gave him thirty 'companions'. Some commentators, rightly I think, suggest that since it appears that these companions were assigned to Samson, rather than invited by him to the party, they probably represented from the Philistine point of view a kind of informal bodyguard to make sure Samson didn't cause any trouble.

Whether or not that is so, it's certain that a man of any

tact or discretion in such a situation of potential domestic tension would have tried his best to keep relationships cordial at the wedding. But what do we find instead? Samson, true to his infantile temperament, gets his thirty companions involved in a ridiculous bet, centring round a totally absurd riddle which he has made up on his way to the banquet.

> 'Let me tell you a riddle,' Samson said to them. 'If you can give me the answer within the seven days of the feast, I will give you thirty linen garments and thirty sets of clothes. If you can't tell me the answer, you must give me thirty linen garments and thirty sets of clothes.'
> 'Tell us your riddle,' they said. 'Let's hear it.'
> He replied,
> > 'Out of the eater, something to eat;
> > out of the strong, something sweet' (14:12–14).

It reminds me of the inane, unanswerable jokes that my children bring home from school; those that are not designed to test the wits at all but to make the other person look thoroughly foolish. One I heard recently went as follows:

> Q : 'How do you keep an idiot waiting?'[*Pause*]
> A : 'I'll tell you later!'

Samson, however, had made the situation much more serious by attaching high stakes to this ridiculous bet: thirty linen garments and thirty sets of clothes. This almost certainly represents the traditional gift that Samson (who, properly speaking, was the host) owed to

92

his thirty male companions. Today we give a present to the bridesmaids; he would have been expected to give a gift to his best men. In other words, Samson is here gambling with his wedding guests to cover the cost of the reception. That's what it comes down to, and it's really in very bad taste.

No wonder that the thirty young men have no intention of letting him get away with it: 'On the fourth day, they said to Samson's wife, "Coax your husband into explaining the riddle for us, or we will burn you and your father's household to death. Did you invite us here to rob us?"' (16:15).

Thus they put pressure on Samson's bride to wheedle the answer out of him; and she does. After all, she is a Philistine and owes loyalty to her own kin. When Samson discovers, however, that his little riddle has been betrayed, instead of accepting the situation with good grace and a friendly chuckle to diffuse the hostile atmosphere (as I feel Jephthah would certainly have done), his immaturity is almost unbelievable.

> Before sunset on the seventh day the men of the town said to him,
>> 'What is sweeter than honey?
>> What is stronger than a lion?'
> Samson said to them,
>> 'If you had not ploughed with my heifer,
>> you would not have solved my riddle.'

Then the Spirit of the LORD came upon him in power. He went down to Ashkelon, struck down thirty of their men, stripped them of their belongings and gave their clothes to those who had explained the riddle. Burning with anger, he went up to his father's

house. And Samson's wife was given to the friend
who had attended him at his wedding (14:18–20).

Observe the petulance and the puerile spite of his reaction. 'Ploughed with my heifer' is frankly a very vulgar
innuendo. In fact the whole couplet rings with the lilting
rhyme you associate with small children's playground
chants. It doesn't take much imagination to visualize
Samson's pouting lips, stamping foot and sulky eyes.

His vicious and unprovoked attack on Ashkelon can
only be called a fit of temper. We've all seen frustrated
children storm into their room, slamming the door
behind them; but we don't expect that kind of behaviour
from adults, still less Spirit-filled he-men. But that's
Samson all over.

And, I'm afraid, it doesn't stop there. There is a sequel
to this story. We're told in 14:19–20 that because Samson
was in such a mood he stormed off, deserted his bride and
never completed the wedding ceremony. As a result the
young lady in question, to avoid the humiliation of being
jilted at the altar, was married instead to one of Samson's
associates. Things like that happened in those days, and
frankly, after his disgraceful behaviour at the wedding, I
don't think Samson could really complain. But of course,
he did.

Later on, at the time of wheat harvest, Samson took a
young goat and went to visit his wife. He said, 'I'm
going to my wife's room.' But her father would not
let him go in.

'I was so sure you thoroughly hated her,' he said,
'that I gave her to your friend. Isn't her younger sis-
ter more attractive? Take her instead' (15:1–2).

94

Within the terms of reference of this ancient culture, a mature person would have accepted this situation. Jacob certainly did when he was done out of a wife in a rather similar fashion. Not Samson! His spiteful sense of humour triumphs again over his good judgment:

> Samson said to them, 'This time I have a right to get even with the Philistines; I will really harm them.' So he went out and caught three hundred foxes and tied them tail to tail in pairs. He then fastened a torch to every pair of tails, lit the torches and let the foxes loose in the standing corn of the Philistines (15:3–5).

It is the sort of cruel, destructive prank one associates with juvenile delinquents. He must have known the fury that such an act of wanton vandalism would provoke. But such violence was meat and drink to Samson. He was an irresponsible mischief-maker.

> When the Philistines asked, 'Who did this?' they were told, 'Samson, the Timnite's son-in-law, because his wife was given to his friend.' So the Philistines went up and burned her and her father to death. Samson said to them, 'Since you've acted like this, I won't stop until I get my revenge on you.' He attacked them viciously and slaughtered many of them (15:6–8).

By verse 15 the day is over and Samson has felled his 1,000 men, using the jawbone of an ass as his only weapon. He celebrates his gruesome blood-bath with another piece of his coarse and infantile humour (15:16). This is our hero, then. A man with so much in his favour, yet so lacking in self-discipline and wisdom as to behave, so often, like a bull on heat. The end is almost inevitable; a man like this is hardly going to settle down with some nice easy-going girl.

Samson in love: Delilah

> Some time later, he fell in love with a woman in the Valley of Sorek whose name was Delilah (16:4).

It does seem that at last Samson may have discovered the difference between love and lust. From the way that the narrator describes this relationship, it appears that for the first time since his broken betrothal, Samson wants some kind of committed relationship. He's fallen in love.

Yet his sensuality, not his good judgment, is still in control. So infatuated is he by the physical attractions of this woman, he is rendered completely blind to the treacherous streak in her character. Not once, not twice, but three times in chapter 16 she tries to betray him to the Philistines.

Was Samson so stupid that he didn't realize that it must be her who had set up the ambush? Was he really fooled by that feigned cry of alarm, 'Samson, the Philistines are on you'? A Judas kiss if ever there was one. Surely he must have realized? Maybe not. Delilah has all the marks of a very shrewd and very clever woman, far cleverer than Samson. It's quite clear she could twist him round her little finger. Remember, we are talking about a treachery that was plotted over the course of years, not just days or weeks. And the demands of passion in a man like Samson blur common sense.

Solomon wrote about the corrosive effects of a whining

woman's tongue. 'A quarrelling wife is like a constant dripping on a rainy day.' It became so eventually with Samson and Delilah. 'With such nagging she prodded him day after day until he was tired to death. So he told her everything' (16:16).

It was not that his strength was magically associated with his hair. Nor was it, as some have suggested, that Samson merely believed his strength was in his hair and so was rendered psychologically impotent by its removal. The text is quite clear. Samson's strength was derived directly from God; it was a supernatural charisma God had sustained in him from his earliest years. He had never known what it was like to be without this charisma. Perhaps he didn't really believe he ever could lose it, it was so much part of him. Perhaps he'd even begun to believe that his unique powers belonged to him in some inalienable way, that the Nazirite vow was a nuisance anyway. He'd broken it often enough in touching dead bodies, after all. He certainly wasn't prepared for the disaster that God brought upon him for breaking the vow.

> Then she called, 'Samson, the Philistines are upon you!'
> He awoke from his sleep and thought, 'I'll go out as before and shake myself free.' But he did not know that the LORD had left him (16:20–21).

Perhaps it was poetic irony that they put out his eyes. After all, it was his eyes that had got him into trouble so often. If only he could have controlled his eyes, he might have been all right. His frivolity could, after all, be amusing at times; even his vindictiveness, in that violent era, maybe could be forgiven. But there was no excuse nor any

97

painless remedy for his intemperate sensuality. In the end, he paid for it in the most humiliating way imaginable.

That is a theme that the author wants us to pick up. Though he does not explicitly draw moralizing lessons out from Samson's life, he surely intends us to discern them, and to learn that those who are tyrannized by their sexual appetites will come to ruin.

Today the sexual expectations of men and women are being elevated to quite ridiculous heights. We are being brainwashed by novels, films and TV soap operas into basing our estimate of our own self-worth on the competence of our sexual performance or the variety of our sexual experience. Our eyes, like Samson's, are daily being subtly trained by a thousand adverts to assess the desirability of the opposite sex in purely physical terms.

In the old days, the persistent pastoral problem was sexual guilt. These days you have a problem in getting people to feel guilty at all about their sexual behaviour.

Learn from Samson. Sex isn't everything. Undisciplined sexual appetites will surely bring you to ruin.

Failure need not be the end of everything

> But the hair on his head began to grow again ... (16:22)

Perhaps as you have been reading these pages you have been feeling completely discouraged. Perhaps, like Samson, you have had great opportunities in life but have wasted them. Perhaps you feel that you too are on the scrap heap, in the darkness of that Philistine jail, with no-one to blame but yourself. Perhaps, like Samson, you have allowed sexual passion to dominate your life and are beginning to experience the self-destructive consequences of that lack of self-discipline. Perhaps, like Samson in his Philistine cell, you feel that the Lord has left you; you feel spiritually deserted.

In your case, the final theme of this story is one of great hope.

Our failures are not God's failures

Look back again to the beginning of the story. 'His parents did not know that this was from the LORD, who was seeking an occasion to confront the Philistines; for at that time they were ruling over Israel' (14:4). We have already noticed that our author very rarely interjects that kind of interpretative comment. Most of the time he leaves the text open for *you* to interpret it. But here it is such an important insight that he is afraid we will miss it if he does not spell it out. He wants us to know, even if Samson's parents did not know, that the whole business of Samson and the Philistine girl was woven by divine providence.

Some people take 14:4 to mean that Samson was deliberately seeking a Philistine bride, so that he could have an opportunity to weaken the Philistine military hold on Israel. I must say, I think that's a most optimistic reading. The whole of Samson's story demonstrates that he never does anything except out of essentially self-centred, hedonistic motives. He chose the Philistine girl for no other reason than that he desired her physically. What the inspired author is pointing out to us, however, is that in

99

spite of the lack of nobility of motive and in spite of Samson's frivolous and sensual nature, God had a purpose in it all and was working out his will, even through such a man.

I have sometimes heard people say, 'We must be holy vessels before God can use us. If we're not holy, God can't use us.' I believe that's wrong. The reason we are to be holy is not so that God can use us, but so that we can be *fit* for his use. God is never limited by our unholiness. If he had to wait to find clean vessels, he would never be able to do anything in this fallen world. He regularly uses sinners. The classic example for the Christian in that respect is the cross, where human wickedness did its worst, but God was achieving his eternal counsel. Oh, he may be disappointed by our sins, bitterly disappointed; but he is never surprised by them. He is never thwarted. Indeed, he anticipates and exploits our failures.

That ought to be an immense encouragement to us. Some of us have made big mistakes that, when we remember them, make us groan inwardly. That does not mean that our life is now a write-off so far as God is concerned, nor – as I have heard some people say – that we are condemned to be 'God's second-best'. He has been working his sovereign purpose out, even in the midst of all our weaknesses and mistakes. Our failures are not his failures.

Our failures need never be the last word

'Then Samson prayed to the LORD' (16:28). Have we ever heard Samson pray to the Lord before? I think you will find that this is a wholly new experience for our hero.

Sadly, the vindictiveness is still there. It would have been nice if Samson's motivation in his last Herculean exploit had been a little less motivated by personal revenge – 'Let me get revenge ... for my two eyes' – and a little more concerned for the honour of God's name over the idols of Philistia. His exploit would have been nobler if his motives had been nobler. But at least Samson is at last being serious. At last he is being spiritual. At last he is praying. Sometimes it takes a great deal to bring us to that point of real prayer; sometimes we have to fail very badly. But such failure never needs to be the last word. In fact, paradoxically, it is only when like Samson we are humbled by failure, and become aware, perhaps for the first time, of our natural inability, that God really has the opportunity to work savingly in our hearts.

There was a man in the New Testament who had to be blinded before he could hear God's voice and ask God's forgiveness. And it was he who wrote:

> But he said to me, 'My grace is sufficient for you, for my power is made perfect in weakness.' Therefore I will boast all the more gladly about my weaknesses, so that Christ's power may rest on me. That is why, for Christ's sake, I delight in weaknesses ... for when I am weak, then I am strong (2 Corinthians 12:9).

Of course you fail. We have all failed; we are all embarrassed by the memories of those failures. Thank God, the church is not an academy for perfect saints but a hospital for sinful failures. Failure is never the end of everything. Sometimes, with the help of Jesus Christ, it can be the beginning.

101

4

A society in decline
Judges 17 – 21

> In those days Israel had no king; everyone did as he
> saw fit (21:25).

It is a truism that the rivers of history run red with blood.
But why do they do so? Humankind has always dreamed
of achieving a world where there is no more violence, no
more war. Throughout the centuries, that dream has fired
human imagination but has never yet come true. Indeed,
our twentieth century has probably witnessed more
bloody carnage than any century that has preceded it.
Why are we so incorrigibly violent? Why are we so unable
to solve our social problems without recourse to war?

It is not a new question; people have always asked it. In
fact I suspect that it was on the mind of the author of this
book of Judges. Ancient Israel, too, had lived through
centuries of bloodshed. Ever since her people had
emerged from their nomadic wanderings in the desert to

settle in the land of Canaan between the Jordan and the Mediterranean Sea, her history had been repeatedly punctuated by war. In early days, the wars were fought against other tribes that challenged Israel's territorial ambitions in the area. We have seen that a cyclical pattern, which our author has described for us, emerged during that period. Periods of peace alternate with periods of prosperity; periods of military conflict alternate with periods of foreign domination.

It could be argued that warfare in that situation was unavoidable. Israel had to defend herself against people like the Midianites and the Philistines, or she simply couldn't have survived as a nation. The armies of Israel were usually outnumbered and those she faced were usually militarily superior. That the battles were won at all, our author regularly ascribes to the fact that God raised up judges to deliver her; charismatically endowed warriors like Gideon and Jephthah and Samson. So our author is certainly no pacifist. He seems to suggest that in situations where foreign armies invaded or oppressed the nation, a war of self-defence, though regrettable, was justified. He clearly believes that God could be trusted to intervene on his people's side in such conflicts.

However, something else was going on during this period of Israel's history. Another pattern was being generated. Not this time a cyclical pattern of war and peace, but a linear pattern of steady decline into spiritual and moral decadence. Violence was very much a part of that pattern, too, only this time there could be no justification for it. If you put those two patterns together, what you get is a downward spiral. And if you have read thus far, you will repeatedly have seen evidence of that spiral throughout the book of Judges.

Take the story of Gideon. He successfully delivered Israel from the Midianites, but in the wake of that triumph he opened the door to a renaissance of idolatry in the country, by erecting that golden oracle which the Jews quickly started to venerate. It is no surprise to be told in 8:33 that no sooner had Gideon died than Israel was immersed in the worship of Canaanite deities once again.

More sinister still is the report in chapter 9 that Abimelech, one of Gideon's many sons, murdered all his brothers in order to secure political power for himself. Even at that early point in the book, one begins to wonder whether a threat even more serious than the Midianites may be lurking within Israel's own boundaries. The same pattern of internal degeneration was detectable again in the story of Jephthah; he, too, successfully delivered Israel, this time from the threat of the Ammonite army. But a foolish vow, owing more to pagan superstition than to faith, led him to commit an act of human sacrifice involving his own daughter. And in an ironic aftermath of his victory over the Ammonites, his Gilead forces engaged in quite unnecessary bloodshed against their fellow-Israelites from Ephraim (12:1–6).

By the time we reach the story of Samson, it has become quite clear that these Spirit-anointed champions, whom God raised up to deliver his people from their enemies, have themselves become part of this pattern of moral decline. For Samson, notwithstanding all his victories over the Philistine menace, is a churlish fool, given to spiteful, adolescent pranks and totally driven by his sex hormones. He offers no spiritual or moral leadership to the nation whatsoever. He's just a solitary Rambo who pursues his own private vendettas. Significantly, after him no more judges appear. The cyclical pattern seems to have come to an end. No more do we hear of God stepping in to turn the tide of history by raising up a judge. Instead, the downward spiral of increasing decadence has straightened out into something perilously close to a vertical free fall.

Before he concludes his book, our author tells us two more stories, intended to illustrate just how rapidly things were going downhill in the country by the end of the period of the judges. They are masterpieces of our author's narrative art, well worth study as examples of Hebrew literature in their own right. The key element they have in common, however, is that unlike the stories of Gideon and Jephthah and Samson, that have dominated the middle parts of the book, there is no foreign threat to Israel's security at all forming a backdrop to these final incidents. These stories are exclusively about the internal state of Israel. And a sorry state it is, as you will see.

Micah

A man named Micah from the hill country of Ephraim said to his mother, 'The eleven hundred shekels of silver that were taken from you and about which I heard you utter a curse – I have that silver with me; I took it.'

Then his mother said, 'The LORD bless you, my son!'

When he returned the eleven hundred shekels of silver to his mother, she said, 'I solemnly consecrate my silver to the LORD for my son to make a carved image and a cast idol. I will give it back to you.'

So he returned the silver to his mother, and she took two hundred shekels of silver and gave them to a silversmith, who made them into the image and the idol. And they were put in Micah's house.

Now this man Micah had a shrine, and he made an ephod and some idols and installed one of his sons as his priest (17:1–5).

In these five very compressed opening verses our author explains to us how it was that this man Micah came to have a private shrine in his own home. It was from the start a morally and theologically dubious situation. He had stolen a very large sum of money from his mother. She, it seems, partly no doubt to expedite its recovery, had announced that the sum had actually been consecrated to God, and since that made it God's property, a divine curse was sure to rest on anybody who had stolen it. Thereupon Micah, who was rather superstitious, decided he had better give the cash back; upon which his mother generously renounced the curse: 'The LORD bless you, my son!'

So far, so good. But we soon discover that Micah's mother is as theologically ill-informed as her superstitious son, for she immediately proceeds to reconsecrate the money for the purpose of constructing an idolatrous shrine, complete with silver image. Indeed, judging from verse 5, the shrine that results from this financial investment had a number of valuable objects in it for the purpose of religious devotion, all of course strictly prohibited by the covenant law of Moses.

Not satisfied with his shrine, however, Micah went on to install one of his own sons as priest to this private cult. This too was a totally irregular procedure, since according to Moses only members of the tribe of Levi could function as priests. To his credit, Micah seems to have recognized this breach of orthodoxy and that no doubt explains what happens next:

> A young Levite from Bethlehem in Judah, who had been living within the clan of Judah, left that town in search of some other place to stay. On his way he came to Micah's house in the hill country of Ephraim.
>
> Micah asked him, 'Where are you from?'
>
> 'I'm a Levite from Bethlehem in Judah,' he said, 'and I'm looking for a place to stay.'
>
> Then Micah said to him, 'Live with me and be my father and priest, and I'll give you ten shekels of silver a year, your clothes and your food' (17:7–10).

Superficially, Micah's intentions here were arguably good. He realized that his son was not a proper priest, and he leapt at the opportunity to secure the services of somebody more kosher. But once again, the whole thing reeks of heresy. What sort of priest hires himself out to a private individual in this fashion, in biblical religion anyway? And what sort of person thinks he or she can manipulate God into guaranteeing them prosperity, by such a mercenary arrangement? It is quite clear that prosperity was the motivating force in Micah's mind:

Then Micah installed the Levite, and the young man became his priest and lived in his house. And Micah said, 'Now I know that the LORD will be good to me, since this Levite has become my priest' (17:12–13).

Micah's actions throughout owe far more to superstition than to biblical faith. Typically, our author does not spell out his disapproval; but, in a way characteristic of Old Testament narrative at its literary best, he simply goes on in chapter 18 to tell us the sequel, and invites us quietly to draw our own conclusions.

A spying party of five Israelites from the tribe of Dan appears on the scene; they and their clans have not yet secured a territorial base in Canaan, so they are on the lookout for vacant property. Passing by Micah's place they hear an unfamiliar southern accent. On enquiring, they discover it belongs to the young priest from Bethlehem. Delighted to have the services of this bona-fide divine oracle so unexpectedly available, they consult him for advice on their hunt for a suitable homeland. 'Don't worry,' says the priest. 'God says you're on to a winner.' And with that divine endorsement ringing in their ears, the spies continue in their search for a suitable homeland for their people.

> So the five men left and came to Laish, where they saw that the people were living in safety, like the Sidonians, unsuspecting and secure. And since their land lacked nothing, they were prosperous. Also, they lived a long way from the Sidonians and had no relationship with anyone else (18:7).

A quiet, remote town, populated by Sidonian merchants

without an army or access to defensive support from Sidon itself or any other ally – to these land-hungry Danites, Laish looked like a juicy sitting duck; a little like Kuwait before the militaristic ambitions of Saddam Hussein, perhaps.

But God had never given the Israelites any mandate to attack Sidonians, nor at this time did Sidon pose any military threat to Israel's borders. The Sidonians were a peaceful, mercantile people. They had no reason to fear anyone, for in general their activities prospered the lands where they lived through their economic activity. They had no enemies, they thought. So although Laish might have been a sitting duck, she was not, according to biblical law, fair game.

The only thing that might have given the Danites a bad conscience about seizing such a city would have been some consideration about what God thought about it. But a priest with a silver oracle had assured them that they need fear no divine disapproval. They were on to a winner, and so when they returned home to their clans and reported the results of their reconnaissance, the decision is grimly predictable.

When they returned to Zorah and Eshtaol, their brothers asked them, 'How did you find things?' They answered, 'Come on, let's attack them! We have seen that the land is very good. Aren't you going to do something? Don't hesitate to go there and take it over. When you get there, you will find an unsuspecting people and a spacious land that God has put into your hands ...' (18:8–10).

109

The abduction of the shrine

En route to performing this piece of ethnic cleansing, the Danite militia once again passed by Micah's home. The five spies told their colleagues about Micah's shrine with the valuable silver image and the priest who had given them such helpful advice. Plunder being their business, the Danites reasoned that Micah's idols were far too good to be monopolized by him alone. They decide to take them into public ownership – without compensation, of course. As for the young Levite, they stifled whatever muted objections he might be murmuring by giving him an offer he couldn't refuse: promotion from ministering at Micah's pathetic little private chapel, to a major tribal shrine at the new provincial capital of Dan, which they would shortly be constructing on the ruins of Laish.

The priest – as one might expect from his previous record of financial self-interest – is lured by the prospect of a sizeable rise in salary. In 18:22–26 we are presented with the rather comic scene of Micah and his household racing after the Danite forces to complain about their outrageous breach of the law of private property. 'You've stolen my gods and my priest,' wails Micah, in the injured tone of a child asking a bigger boy if he can have his ball back. 'You'd better keep your mouth shut,' reply the bullying Danites. 'Some of our warriors have a rather short fuse, you know; we wouldn't want anyone getting hurt, would we?'

The pathetic Micah began by stealing his mother's silver, and at the end of the story is left empty-handed, himself the victim of theft. It is one of those little ironies that our author loves.

And the poor Sidonians?

Then [the Danites] took what Micah had made, and his priest, and went on to Laish, against a peaceful and unsuspecting people. They attacked them with the sword and burned down their city. There was no-one to rescue them because they lived a long way from Sidon and had no relationship with anyone else (18:27–28).

Do you see how, in the eloquence of simple narrative, our author expresses the shame he feels over what has taken place? The Danites do not even seem to have offered peace terms, as the law of Moses required. It was a ruthless surprise attack, totally unprovoked, and they had taken no prisoners.

Our author has just one more observation to add to our general sense of unease at this whole incident. He could have told us much earlier, but with the storyteller's eye to maximizing audience impact he leaves it until the very end of chapter 18.

There the Danites set up for themselves the idols, and Jonathan son of Gershom, the son of Moses, and his sons were priests for the tribe of Dan until the time of the captivity of the land (18:30).

Well, now, there's a shock! He knew his name all along, but didn't tell us. Micah's priest was none other than a grandson of Moses.

A pious Jewish scribe was, it seems, so outraged by this suggestion that he inserted a letter 'n' in the ancient manuscript to make it read 'son of Manasseh', rather than of Moses. Some English versions follow that reading, but there are very strong reasons for accepting the rendering of the NIV; that it is Moses, not Manasseh, who is in view here. Could there be any clearer evidence of the decadence of Israelite religion than that the direct descendants of Moses himself were now ministering at a shrine that was corrupted by superstition and idolatry, in a city that had been captured in total defiance of Moses' moral law?

Tacitly, you see, our author is showing us that the downward spiral had turned into a vertical slide. But as a Hollywood director would say, you ain't seen nothing yet. Micah's tale is an amusing farce compared to the barbarism with which Judges concludes.

The Levite's concubine

> Now a Levite who lived in a remote area in the hill country of Ephraim took a concubine from Bethlehem in Judah (19:1).

It is interesting that once more the leading characters originate in Bethlehem, and once more the story features a Levite. Possibly our author feels there is some connection with the story of Micah. Could this Levite of chapter 19 be none other than Jonathan, Moses' grandson? The text doesn't say so. But it does tell us that he lived in a remote area of the hill country of Ephraim, just like Micah did. So the possibility is there.

> [He] took a concubine from Bethlehem in Judah. But she was unfaithful to him. She left him and went back to her father's house in Bethlehem, Judah. After she had been there for four months, her husband went to her to persuade her to return. He had with him his

servant and two donkeys. She took him into her father's house, and when her father saw him, he gladly welcomed him (19:1–3).

We have seen already that in the ancient world a concubine was a kept mistress who remained legally part of her parents' family and therefore enjoyed none of the rights that a wife possessed in law. Scholars are unsure whether the text implies that this concubine actually had an affair with some other man, or whether there was just a domestic quarrel. Whichever it was, the result was that she went home to mother, or in this case to father. The Levite, annoyed by her desertion, eventually went after her, intending to woo her back. At her home in Bethlehem he met her father; the two men seem to have struck up an immediate liking for each other. In fact, they spent the next five days in one long stag party, with plenty of good food and drink to help the convivial atmosphere along. Every time the Levite began to think he ought to be making tracks for home, his host dissuaded him. Indeed, by the fifth day, the Levite must have been saying to himself, 'If I don't leave now I never will.'

So it was that he, his concubine and his servant ended up leaving Bethlehem, rather late in the evening, for the long journey back north. They came to the town of Jebus, a city that David would later capture and rename Jerusalem. But at that time, Jebus was still a pagan fortress. Though the Levite considered seeking refuge for the night there, he dismissed the idea, feeling it would be unsafe. So he travelled on in the sparse remaining daylight to reach Gibeah, an Israelite town, in the tribal territory of Benjamin. Ironically, as it transpired, he would have been better advised to seek pagan hospitality in Jebus.

As soon as they arrive in Gibeah, one senses that something is very wrong. There is a sinister look in everybody's eye as this small party sits on their suitcases in the town square. Nobody offers them accommodation for the night – which was a reprehensible breach of etiquette in the ancient Middle East, as indeed it still is today. Could it be that people from 'up north' were not welcome down in the south, in Benjamin? Eventually, one old man takes pity on them. Significantly, he is not a local Benjamite but a northerner, like them. 'For goodness' sake', he says, in a tone that sounds disturbingly like a warning, 'don't spend the night in the square, whatever you do.'

Later that evening, the reason for his anxiety becomes quite plain.

The outrage committed

> While they were enjoying themselves [in his home], some of the wicked men of the city surrounded the house. Pounding on the door, they shouted to the old man who owned the house, 'Bring out the man who came to your house so we can have sex with him' (19:22).

The Levite escaped homosexual rape by this lewd mob – but only because he threw his own concubine out of the door, as a substitute sex object for them upon which to spend their violent lust. After a night of what must have been horrifyingly vicious sexual abuse, the poor woman staggered back to the old man's dwelling. She never managed even to knock on the door. When the Levite opened the door at dawn he discovered her dead body on the doorstep. 'He said to her, "Get up; let's go."

But there was no answer' (18:28).

Now what he does next sounds quite bizarre to our ears. It is almost like a scene from a horror film.

> The man put her [corpse] on his donkey and set out for home. When he reached home, he took a knife and cut up his concubine, limb by limb, into twelve parts and sent them into all the areas of Israel. Everyone who saw it said, 'Such a thing has never been seen or done, not since the day the Israelites came up out of Egypt. Think about it! Consider it! Tell us what to do!' (19:28–30).

To understand what is happening here you have to realize that Israel was a federation of tribes, united by a blood covenant. In an ancient covenant, a sacrificial animal was sometimes cut in pieces as a witness to the seriousness of the mutual promise that the parties were making. The logic of such a sacrifice may well have been that those who participated in the covenant were taking upon themselves a kind of self-invoked curse – 'If I break the terms of this covenant relationship, then may God make me like this slaughtered animal.'

Do you see what the Levite is doing, then, by this macabre piece of theatre? He is using his concubine's severed corpse as a gruesome reminder to the twelve tribes of Israel of the allegiance they owed to the blood of their national covenant. He is summoning the Israelite tribal muster by the most powerful of symbols; but he's doing so this time not in order to face some external aggressor, some Philistine, Ammonite or Midianite army as earlier generations did. He is doing it to seek justice in a matter of civil dispute with a tribe from their own number.

115

The outrage avenged

His appeal was successful. 'Then all the Israelites from Dan to Beersheba and from the land of Gilead came out as one man and assembled before the LORD in Mizpah' (20:1). That the Levite's protest could command that kind of wide response strongly suggests, I think, that he was a man of considerable influence, and possibly reinforces the suspicion that he may well have been Archbishop Jonathan from the new diocese of Dan in the north. But if so, the Levite displays none of grandfather Moses' political prudence. He makes it quite clear that he expects vengeance on the inhabitants of Gibeah for this outrage. And the tribes, at least eleven of them, agree. The tribe of Benjamin, to which Gibeah belonged, remains loyal to its fellow clansmen. They refuse to give up the gang of rapists responsible for the crime, and instead make it quite clear that they are prepared to fight for their right to administer justice independent of such interference by the other tribes. The result is that the whole affair escalates into a full-scale civil war.

Our author's account of the fighting that follows is a masterpiece. He tells how it took three days for the federal army of Israel to capture Gibeah, and by the end the total body count was numbered in tens of thousands. What's more, in a quite unnecessary punitive atrocity, the entire civilian population of the town of Gibeah was put to the sword, including women and children. Quite frankly, it smacks of something disturbingly like some modern genocidal campaigns of violence in Bosnia or Rwanda.

In a final ironic postscript in chapter 21, our author describes how, when they had at last cooled off, the

Israelites began to realize they had gone decidedly over the top. In their hot-blooded pursuit of vengeance, they had virtually eliminated the whole tribe of Benjamin. The famous twelve tribes could be reduced to eleven, a much less propitious number. Somehow they must retrieve the situation; practically speaking, that meant finding some women to become wives of the tattered remnants of the Benjamite army, whose own women, you remember, had been slaughtered. But there was a problem in finding such women. The families of Israel had taken an oath, at the time of the tribal muster at Mizpah, that in view of what had happened to the Levite's concubine they would never again give their daughters in marriage to a man of Benjamin. 'We can't break our promise now, can we?' they reasoned. 'So how do we get out of this?'

'Oh,' said someone, 'it's easy. We took another vow at Mizpah as well, don't you remember? We made a lot of vows there. We also agreed that anybody who didn't support us in the fight against Benjamin would be put to death. Well, I happen to know that absolutely nobody took part in the civil war from Jabesh Gilead. So all we have to do is go over there, put all the men and women in that city to death in fulfilment of our second vow, but spare the unmarried daughters this time. Then we can invite the remnant of Benjamin to help themselves. Since they are not our daughters, we will not be breaking our first vow, you see.'

So that's what they did.

Nor was this the end of the tortuous contortions of their moral logic. Unfortunately, there weren't quite enough virgins in Jabesh Gilead to go round. A few Benjamite veterans still lacked a wife. So someone had another bright idea: 'At the next harvest festival, just tell the Benjamites to abduct any available young female they fancy. We'll just undertake to turn a blind eye to it. Everyone knows these things happen at harvest time. And since we're not actually giving the girls to them, we shan't be breaking our vow.'

Once again, our author doesn't spell out his horror at these crazy antics. He leaves us, his readers, to draw our own conclusions. But it isn't difficult to sense once again the shame and exasperation he feels, that the history of his people should be chequered with such acts of unfettered violence and moral blindness. Silently he asks the question 'Why? Why is it that history goes this way?'

His tacit answer perhaps lies in recognizing that nothing that happens in these two stories is new. There is in fact a disturbing, ironic resonance with some earlier Bible stories. The rape of the Levite's concubine, for instance, has a number of clear parallels to an incident in the life of Abraham's nephew, Lot, recorded in Genesis 19. There are a number of reasons for believing that our author is deliberately evoking resonances with that older story in the way he tells his story. Significantly, however, the city in question that time was not Gibeah but Sodom, the most notorious hell-hole in all history. The implication is embarrassingly plain. The kind of things that Hebrew storybooks associated with Sodom were now becoming commonplace in Israelite cities. And the tribes seemed unable to find either the moral resolve or the judicial wisdom to eliminate such crime from the community, without unleashing totally disproportionate forces of violence that threatened to undermine the political unity of the whole country. Identify the reason for the degeneration of Sodom, then, and you may have the diagnosis of Israel's social sickness too. It is a sickness, of course, that is far from unfamiliar to us. We have read stories like these in our newspapers again and again within the last few years. And they provoke in us the same question. Why? Why is it that we human beings are incapable of resolving social problems without recourse to violence?

Our author believes that he knows the answer. I have pointed out a number of times that he is reluctant to interject interpretative comments into his narrative. He prefers, like all great storytellers, to involve us in the narrative and invite us to draw our own conclusions. But four times in these concluding chapters he departs from his normal practice and inserts an interpretative comment of his own. These interruptions are all the more significant because they are so rare, and because each time, his comment is identical. 'In those days Israel had no king; everyone did as he saw fit' (17:6); 'In those days Israel had no king' (18:1); 'In those days Israel had no king' (19:1); and most significant of all, for it is the postscript to the entire book: 'In those days Israel had no king; everyone did as he saw fit' (21:25).

Here, according to the inspired historian, is the reason for Israel's sorry decline. It was the lack of a monarchy.

Can he be serious? We British know something about the monarchy, and most of us are a bit disillusioned about it at the moment. Is he really suggesting that a royal dynasty is the magic cure for the kind of moral and spiritual decay that he has been illustrating in these stories? Clearly law and order was at a low ebb in Israel. A king would provide a centralized source of authority that arguably, at least, could counteract anarchic elements in the society. So in that sense there is a certain wisdom in what he says.

But he is surely not so naive as to believe that the political institution of monarchy is incorruptible. Certainly, any later Jewish reader would have known, from painful experience, that kings were no more a solution to that downward spiral than the judges had been. Idolatry, social injustice, criminal violence, sexual immorality, civil war – all these things are features of the later history of Israel, and her kings play no small part in their prominence. No, our author is not naive about monarchy. This fourfold comment of his has to be read against the background of the books of Samuel and Kings, to which I think he is quite consciously contributing his own historical record. When you set it against that background, you realize that he has a particular style of monarchy in mind. I suspect, indeed, that he has a particular king in mind. And I suspect that he has given us a subtle clue to that king's identity in the geographical association of these two stories: Bethlehem.

The next book in the Bible continues to find in Bethlehem a focus of interest. We will discover there that amidst the sordid and violent days of the judges, not everybody was locked into the pursuit of self-interest. A girl called Ruth – significantly, of pagan parentage – was quietly demonstrating to Israel a nobler lifestyle than the soap opera of sex and violence that seems to have been the norm in the rest of the country. She was destined to become the great-grandmother of the king our author is looking for – David. Bethlehem would be his birthplace.

Set this book against the background of the entire Bible and it is clear that what our author is really getting at is this: the root problem of human beings is that we do not want to be ruled. We want to follow our own devices; as Frank Sinatra sang, we want to do it our way. We have our religious ideas, just as Micah did, and we want to express them. We have our ambitions, just as the Danites did, and we want to pursue them. We have our sexual desires, just as the men of Gibeah did, and we want to satisfy them. We have our ideas of justice, just as the tribal muster at Mizpah did, and we want to execute them. What we do not want to do is to bow our necks to the rule of God.

Oh, God's all right if he keeps his place, baptizing our enterprises with reassuring promises of blessing. But a God who has ideas of his own, plans of his own, desires of his own, justice of his own – a God like that might collide with our ideas, ambitions, desires and justice. We don't want that. We want to do as we see fit.

This is what the Bible as a whole means by 'sin'. It is not just a label we attach to certain kinds of prohibited acts. In the Bible, sin is a mindset of moral independence, a refusal to submit to the sovereign rule of God over our lives. All the acts of criminal and anarchistic violence for which this world mourns are the result of such sin. The reason the river of history runs red with blood is sin; and there is no simple answer to it. That sin principle, that idiosyncratic moral independence, is embedded in our social conditioning and in our genetic make-up. We cannot escape it.

We've been like that, says the Bible, since the infancy of our race. What's the answer?

The answer, says our author, is a king. Not just any king, but a king like David, born in Bethlehem as David was, but greater even than he. For, the sacred historian will go on to tell us, even David had his faults. Even he was a man of blood. The king we need must be a king who somehow stands outside this heritage of wilful, sinful rebellion that the rest of us share. No human judge, no

121

human king, could deliver us, though in all of these stories the Bible is preparing us for the thought that such a deliverer is what we need. What did he announce when he began his public ministry? 'The kingdom of heaven is near.' That is what he had come to bring. And how did he bring it? Not by the violence of war, but by becoming himself, like the severed corpse of the concubine, a bloody sign of the broken covenant. By his cross he summons us, not to war, but to repentance.

5

Ruth: a woman of character

Ruth 1

The book of Ruth is one of the most moving stories in the whole biblical canon. Many people think it shows such sensitivity that it must have been written by a woman. If that is so, I think it may well have been the wife of the author of the book of Judges! For there are a great many theological connections between the two books. As we begin our study, why not read the whole of it first, and discover for yourself what a beautifully told story it is.

Lament

There's a hole in the world now. In the place where he was, there's now just nothing ... Only a gap remains ... There's nobody now who saw just what he saw, knows what he knew, remembers what he remembered, loves what he loved. A person, an irreplaceable person, is gone ... Questions I have can never now get answers. The world is emptier. My son is gone. Only a hole remains, a void, a gap, never to be filled.

Nicholas Wolterstoff teaches philosophy at Yale. In June 1983, his 25-year-old son Eric died in a climbing accident in the Alps. In *Lament for a Son* (1987), Professor Wolterstoff tried to trace the personal anguish of his loss as he struggled to come to terms with it. Some of you who are reading now, I imagine, have travelled that path too; perhaps are travelling it at this moment. If so, you will know the stages of grief that he chronicles in his book: the numbness of the early days, that others too often mistake for strength; the deep sadness that engulfs the spirit once that initial shock wears off, drowning it in wave upon wave of melancholy and depression; the irrational feelings of guilt and anger that surprise and bewilder the mourner; the strange struggle between fantasy and reality, the tormenting expectation that he will at some moment come through the door and everything will be back as it was before; the ache that finds no relief; the questions that find no answers; the regrets, the yearning for just one more opportunity to say sorry, to say thank you, maybe just to say good-bye.

And the utter sense of isolation, that private hell which is so exasperated by well-intentioned but wholly inadequate platitudes, often from well-meaning Christians: 'You'll get over it,' they say, when you're screaming for someone to articulate just how appallingly grim it feels. 'You have your memories,' they say, but you don't want memories. Memories are just dust and ashes in your mouth, merely the trigger for fresh pain. A phrase of music, a fragrance in the air, a passing likeness in the crowds; such insignificant and unplanned souvenirs, yet they're more than sufficient to plunge the soul down fresh cataracts of despair. 'There's a hole in the world now, a void, a gap, never to be filled,' writes Wolterstoff. And for those who have loved, that hole passes right through the heart.

If you have journeyed that path of grief, you're going to have no problem in engaging emotionally with the story of Ruth. For it too is the story of bereavement, of two women thrown into a situation of utter hopelessness and despair by the death of their loved ones.

The opening lines set the stage in history for this domestic tragedy. 'In the days when the judges ruled ...' We know from our earlier studies what our narrator intends us to conclude from that. The time of the judges was the time when there was no law in Israel, when everyone did as he pleased. The time of the judges was the time when innocent young girls got raped on city streets and were left for dead on doorsteps!

It would have been a tough enough period at the best of times. But to the violence and the criminality of that period, our narrator adds a second burden; a cruelty of providence. Not only was it the day when the judges ruled, there was famine in the land. Was this a judgment from God upon the people's moral degeneracy? Was it perhaps, as we have seen in parts of Africa in recent years, a famine exacerbated by incessant warmongering? I suspect our narrator may intend us to draw some such inference, because Bethlehem is the setting for his story, and Bethlehem was the very place from which that gang-rape of Judges 19 emerges. It's ironic too because the word Bethlehem means 'the house of bread'. There was no bread in the house of bread. Is it any wonder, in a place where sexual brutality and mob violence had become commonplace?

Still, Bethlehem was at least, as the narrator records, a city of Judah. That is, it lay within the tribal boundaries of the Promised Land, the land which God had given to his chosen people. So once again, one cannot but detect at least a hint that Elimelech's decision, to forsake Bethlehem as an economic refugee, and go to Moab was ill-judged. Moab was hardly the place where any self-respecting Jew would choose to live. They were idolatrous pagans in Moab, and had made no secret of their enmity towards Israel throughout the preceding centuries. In fact, the law of God, the book of Deuteronomy, said, 'No Moabite shall enter the Lord's assembly' (see Deuteronomy 23:3). True, it was not strictly speaking illegal, or contrary to the terms of God's covenant law, for Elimelech to move his family to Moab in time of famine. But it was no act of great faith either, especially since he took with him his two (presumably teenage) sons. What chance was there in Moab that they would find Jewish girls to woo? Is it any surprise that we find that Mahlon and Kilion eventually announce their intention to marry local Moabite women?

I think we can conclude that, like so many at the time of the judges, Elimelech sat pretty loose to the religion of his forefathers. He was not downright apostate maybe, but he fell far short of being a spiritual hero. And as if to confirm that suspicion, the narrator records not only his premature death, but also the premature death of his two sons as well. In an Old Testament context we may be intended to read this too as an act of divine judgment. But be that as it may, with all the men there untimely removed, the stage is cleared for what to Jewish ears must have been a rather unexpected and novel twist in the story. Unlike so many of those militaristic adventures that we read about in the book of Judges surrounding this period of time, this will be a tale all about *women*. Women, what's more, who demonstrate a good deal more spirituality in their little finger than most of the men in the whole period of the book of Judges seem to have had in their entire bodies.

Naomi

> When she heard in Moab that the LORD had come to the aid of his people by providing food for them, Naomi and her daughters-in-law prepared to return home from there. With her two daughters-in-law she left the place where she had been living and set out on the road that would take them back to the land of Judah (1:6–7).

Had Elimelech's widow been a reluctant *émigré* in the first place? She is certainly keen to get back to Judah now. The death of her husband and sons has resulted in the rediscovery of her spiritual roots. She heard that 'the LORD' had provided food for them. That is the way she saw it. Moab had been a huge mistake and the Lord had judged them for it. She had lost everything; she had not even a grandchild to show for it all. 'It's time to go back. Let's try to pretend these ten years have never happened. Let's try to salvage something out of the appalling misery of it all,' she says. But then a thought occurs to her, and she says to her two daughters-in-law, 'Go back, each of you, to your mother's home. May the LORD show kindness to you, as you have shown to your dead and to me' (1:8).

When they married into Elimelech's family, technically Ruth and Orpah became part of that family. There was no longer any legal link back to their parental tribe. But in this rather unusual situation, Naomi sees that their best interests are served by a return to their families in Moab. Many commentators interpret her words as a gesture of rather exceptional generosity in the face of profound personal grief. For Naomi is volunteering to bid farewell to the only remaining social support she has left in her widowed state. We have no idea what kind of extended family may have been back in Bethlehem waiting for her return, but now that she was elderly it could not have been that much. It says much for Naomi's character that her daughters-in-law are so reluctant to take advantage of this offer. 'No,' they tell her in verse 10. 'We will go back with you to your people.'

Perhaps it was partly their solidarity in grief that had drawn these women together. But it has to be said that bereavement doesn't always have that effect on people. We grieve in different ways. Sometimes, the experience of loss has the effect of distancing us from family members rather than drawing us closer to them. In any case, the relationship between a mother-in-law and her sons' wives is not renowned for its easy affection. I think Naomi must have been, at least in the days before her husband's death, a woman of great kindness and affection, amply living up to her name, Naomi, which means 'pleasant'. Her suggestion that Ruth and Orpah should return home was no doubt just one more expression of a graciousness that they had come to expect of her. And their loyalty to her confirms the affection in which she was held as a result.

But I can't help suspecting our narrator wants us to catch an ironic, perhaps even sarcastic edge to her tone in verse 8 when she says, 'May the LORD show kindness to you, as you have shown to your dead and to me,' as if one could detect the unspoken implication: 'God, frankly, could take a lesson from you two; pagans though you are, you've shown a great deal more kindness to me than he has; I just hope he treats you better than he's treated me, that's all. For he has left me without rest, without a home, without a husband to my name, and no prospect of ever finding such security or peace of mind again.'

This cynical edge is even clearer in verse 13: 'It is more bitter for me than for you, because the LORD's hand has gone out against me!' Do you not feel a streak of bitterness there? As if to say, 'Don't stick with me, I'm a loser, I'm a jinx. Things will only get worse for you if you stick with me. After all, what are you? Young, Moabite women. Back where I come from, you'll be victims of all kinds of racial discrimination and sexual harassment. I know what it's like in Bethlehem these days. Your only hope of survival in that jungle is if you've got husbands to protect you and to provide for you. But what hope is there of that for you? What self-respecting Jew is going to take one of that despised Moabite race to wife in their own country? My boys only did it because they were living in Moab. They'd never have done it at home. Maybe if I had more sons, they would do the decent thing and marry you in their brother's place, but I haven't, nor any prospect of getting any, and even if I did, you'd be past marriageable age by the time they were grown up. It's pointless you coming back with me. You'll only increase your store of bad luck. The only hope you have is in Moab. In Judah there's no hope for any of us. Least of all for me. No, my daughters, it is more bitter for me than for you because the Lord's hand has gone out against me.'

Perhaps, then, those commentators are right who suggest that it was not so much heroic generosity on Naomi's part as resigned despair, that moved her to offer these two women the freedom to return to their Moabite homeland; a hopelessness so abject in its grief that it had become almost masochistic in the intensity of its self-pity. That certainly seems to be the mood of her greeting to the women of Bethlehem when she eventually gets back there: '"Don't call me Naomi," she told them. "Call me Mara [that is, bitter], because the Almighty has made my life very bitter. I went away full, but the LORD has brought me back empty. Why call me Naomi? The LORD has afflicted me; the Almighty has brought misfortune upon me"' (1:20–21). It's as if coming back to Bethlehem, with all its old memories, brings out the full force of the anger of this grief-stricken woman.

One translator has tried very poorly to anglicize the pun. 'Don't call me sweetheart, call me sourpuss.' But that is how grief takes us human beings. Beyond the range of hope she is plunged into depths of uncharacteristic melancholy. Professor Wolterstoff again:

I've become an alien in the world, shyly touching it as if it's not mine. I don't belong any more ... The lines of memory leading up to his life in the present, they all enter a place of cold and inky blackness and never come out ... I buried myself that warm June day. It was me those gardeners lowered on squeaking straps into that hot dry hole ... It was me over whom we slid that heavy slab. more than I can lift. It was me on whom we shovelled dirt. It was me we left behind ...

Sometimes I think that happiness is over for me.

A lesson about grieving

Some commentators, recognizing the negative mood of Naomi's dialogue in this chapter, are disposed to criticize her. After all, they say, Ruth was grieving too, but she seems to have found a much more positive frame of mind than her mother-in-law. So, surely the author intends to disparage Naomi's bleak despair. It certainly can't be right to hurl blame upon God in the way that Naomi repeatedly does in verses 13, 20 and 21.

But personally I doubt very much that the narrator intends us to respond in that critical fashion. I suspect that rather like the author of the book of Job, and like the authors of many of the psalms, our author here is simply encouraging us to empathize with the emotional devastation that bereavement brings in its wake. Of course Naomi blames God. Many grief-stricken souls do, and it's easy to see why. Is he not the sovereign ruler of all human affairs? Are life and death not his gift? If he didn't take Elimelech and her two sons away from her, who did? There's no impiety in that kind of emotional honesty.

God in this story is inviting us to be real about our own feelings in similar circumstances. All characterization in a narrative is an invitation to identify with the character. And for some, that identification will be with Naomi. If we have any doubts about the Bible's willingness for us to identify with the kind of anger she displays in her loss and loneliness, even anger directed against God himself, we do well to remember the one who in his hour of grief cried out in identification with suffering innocents the world over, 'My God, my God, why have you forsaken me?'

131

When we are bewildered by God's dealings with us and feel cheated by the cruelty of his providence, then it is natural, and certainly not unspiritual, to want to tell him so. Bottling up our rage in that situation is likely to have only the effect of intensifying our depression.

I have many times had people say to me in such distress, 'I know I shouldn't feel like this.' But 'should' is not a helpful word in the context of our emotional lives. Our feelings are not under the control of our wills in the way that our moral actions are. To be ashamed of your feelings is a little like being ashamed of your appearance. There's only a limited amount you can do to change the way you look. And there's only a limited amount you can do to change the way you feel. The appropriate response to negative feelings is the same as an appropriate response to that pimple that you wish were not on your face: acceptance, not guilt.

If we refuse to face up to our negative feelings, we are very likely to condemn ourselves to an even more vicious cycle of accumulated inner grievance, from which we will find no easy escape.

In his novel *The Blood of the Lamb*, Peter de Vries tells a story that had a very powerful effect on me, when many years ago my daughter was seriously ill. It is about a man whose daughter is dying of leukaemia. On her twelfth birthday, he is making his way to the hospital carrying a birthday cake in his arms. Before he gets there, word reaches him that his daughter has died. He staggers in despair around the streets, still clutching the cake, not knowing where he is going. He finds himself outside a church that has a crucifix on the wall. And suddenly, as he looks up at the crucifix, he explodes with rage and hurls the birthday cake at the face of Christ.

When I first read that, all my evangelical defences were aroused. It was, I told myself, an outrageously blasphemous act. Then I reflected further, and realized that it was nothing of the sort. It was a symbol of anger, true – but what is Jesus on the cross, if he is not a symbol of anger, the passionate anger of God against the evil of this broken and sinful world? That cross is the sign of that divine anger venting itself safely, healingly, in a gigantic catharsis of the divine passion. In that cross, God reconciles himself to a sinful world. There, his anger is discharged. So how could he possibly mind another father, who has also lost a child, venting his anger similarly?

It is an unjust, tragic world in which we live. It so often steals the ones we love best. When we feel angry, as at a time of bereavement, we need to remember that God is no stranger to that emotion. He has felt it too. I don't believe he minds us expressing our anger. I think he knows that we need to get such feelings off our chests if we are ever to be reconciled to what has happened, or indeed be reconciled to him, the architect of our lives. We should not blame others, and I don't believe we should blame ourselves when we feel such negative emotions. All grief is self-pity. We have lost somebody who was important to us. And even the knowledge they are in a happier place and would not return to us if they could, does not take the hole away that passes through the heart.

Naomi's grief will not last for ever. It's important we remember that. This story will have a happy ending. But while the grief does last, there is absolutely nothing in biblical religion that required Naomi to pretend she felt other than she did. And there is every encouragement in biblical religion for her to articulate her sorrow in God's presence, just as she felt it.

133

Yet in this scene of tragedy and brokenness, there is already a sign of hope. Naomi does not recognize it at this point in the story, for it comes from a most unexpected source. We must now look at the other leading lady in the drama.

Ruth

> Then Orpah kissed her mother-in-law good-bye, but Ruth clung to her.
>
> 'Look,' said Naomi, 'your sister-in-law is going back to her people and her gods. Go back with her.'
>
> But Ruth replied, 'Don't urge me to leave you or to turn back from you. Where you go I will go, and where you stay I will stay. Your people will be my people and your God my God. Where you die I will die, and there I will be buried. May the LORD deal with me, be it ever so severely, if anything but death separates you and me' (1:14–17).

Although it occurs early in the plot, this decision on Ruth's part is in fact the hinge upon which the whole story will turn. As events proceed, we shall discover that it is the turning point not only for the fate of Ruth and Naomi themselves, but for the entire nation of Israel. It is not too much to say that God's entire plan of salvation for the whole world hinges on this apparently insignificant decision of a Moabite widow. That's what makes this story so extraordinary.

Why did she refuse to go home? Naomi tried to persuade her, but the force of her logic did not make the slightest dent in Ruth's resolution: 'When Naomi realised that Ruth was determined to go with her, she stopped urging her' (1:18). Literally, 'she refrained from speaking to her'. Once again, the tone of the Hebrew suggests not so much gratitude for Ruth's fidelity as the exasperated, even sullen, silence of one whose ability to fight has been drained to nothing by her emotional devastation.

Naomi is beyond caring. She doesn't believe that Ruth's grand gesture is going to make any difference to her situation. As far as she's concerned it is utter folly, and rationally speaking she is right to think so. Ruth had every justification for going back to her own familiar world, as her sister-in-law Orpah had chosen to do. It was the sensible, expected thing to do; nobody could possibly blame her. Even her mother-in-law was saying so. Yet she opts to stay with Naomi, knowing that in all probability she is opting for a life of poverty, celibacy and exile. Why did she make that choice?

For our author, the key is clearly to be found in Ruth's own words. 'Don't urge me to leave you or to turn back from you. Where you go I will go, and where you stay I will stay. Your people will be my people and your God my God ...' (1:16–17).

What do those words imply?

At the very least, they imply that Ruth has clearly become a believer in the God of the Bible. She may be a Moabitess by race, but her faith has now become the faith of a Hebrew, not just nominally because she had married into a Jewish family, but in her own right. When she is given the opportunity to go back to her old tribal gods she makes a personal decision not to do so. Clearly, the faith that she had embraced meant something personally to her. I think that must testify to Naomi's godly example. It is very hard to believe that Ruth had learned much about biblical religion from her husband or her father-in-law that would have attracted her to it. It must have been this gracious lady Naomi who had made the spiritual impact on Ruth's life.

There's an interesting subtlety in the narrator's use of that verb 'return'. In Hebrew it carries the sense not only of turning back physically, but also the metaphorical sense of 'repent' or 'convert': in other words, it can have the meaning of turning to God. And it carries that sense here, for Ruth is not returning to Bethlehem physically; she's never been there. Yet the Hebrew text of verse 22 distinctly says, 'Both Naomi returned and Ruth returned.' This was not just a journey for Ruth, you see. It was a baptism. Ruth's decision to accompany her mother-in-law to Bethlehem was a public identification with the God of Israel. 'Your God will be my God,' she had vowed. That desire not to identify any longer with the pagan idols of her own people was a major factor, it seems, in Ruth's choice.

Yet there is more to it, I think, even than that. Ruth's words in verses 16 and 17 are not merely a simple affirmation. She quite deliberately casts her decision into the form of a covenant promise. The invocation of a curse upon herself, should she break her word, is characteristic of such covenants in the ancient world. 'May the LORD deal with me, be it ever so severely, if anything but death separates you and me.' Such a form of words in the ancient world had the uncompromising force of a legal contract, rather similar to a marriage vow today – 'for better or worse, till death us do part'. Even more remarkable is the similarity between the form of words that Ruth chooses to use, and the covenant promise that God had made to Israel at the time of Moses. God had said to Israel repeatedly in the earlier books of the Bible, 'Wherever you go, my presence will go with you.' And what does Ruth say to Naomi? 'Where you go I will go, where you stay I will stay.' God had said to Israel again and again, 'I will be your God and you will be my people.' And what does Ruth say to Naomi? 'Your people will be my people and your God will be my God.'

The parallels are conspicuous, and are surely deliberate. Why does Ruth do it? Why should she bind herself so irrevocably and solemnly to this other woman, in a hallowed form of words so characteristic of the divine covenant?

I believe it is because our author is inviting us to draw a quite obvious conclusion. Ruth may have been a new believer in the God of Israel, but she had already learned that the primary moral response which the God of Israel demanded of his people was a covenant love like his own; a covenant love evidenced not just by fidelity in our relationship to him, but also by fidelity in our relationships with one another. And that was the very thing that was breaking down in this period when the judges ruled.

Hosea, a few centuries later, would complain about the same thing. 'There is no faithfulness, no covenant love, and no acknowledgment of God in the land.' Instead, he says, 'there is only cursing, lying, murder, stealing and adultery. They break all bounds, and bloodshed follows bloodshed; and because of this', he says, 'the land mourns, and all who live in it waste away' (see Hosea 4:1-2).

He was describing eighth-century Israel, but he could just as well have been describing the earlier period of the judges. Israel was sinking in a sea of moral anarchy, and at the root of that collapse was a collapse of the very idea of covenant love in personal relationships. People didn't care about one another any more. People didn't trust one another any more. People weren't faithful to one another any more. God had promised such covenant love to them, but Israel for her part, in her rebelliousness, saw nothing to be gained by demonstrating such love towards one another, and she was reaping the judgment of God through her callous selfishness. The land mourned. There was no bread, even in the house of bread.

And yet here, in a private exchange between two apparently quite insignificant women, a different pattern of human relationships emerges. Ruth, the pagan convert, is showing a true-born Jewess precisely the kind of covenant love-commitment that God requires of his people when it comes to relationships. Orpah her sister-in-law was not a specially bad person for failing to demonstrate the same devotion to Naomi. She just wasn't a believer. She wasn't able to take the step of faith Ruth had taken. It was too sacrificial for her. She didn't believe in this God who rewarded covenant love. But Ruth did. And that's why Ruth chose the way she did.

That is the lesson our author wants us to draw from this story. When we human beings abandon love for God and neighbour, we make a desert around ourselves in which often the weak and the vulnerable like Naomi suffer most, even though they may be the least guilty. And yet when just one individual discovers the faith with which to make that costly sacrifice of themselves that love for God and neighbour demands, then judgment begins to lift, the desert begins to blossom, and despair begins to give way to hope.

Ruth's decision to cling to Naomi was indeed a watershed. From it would result not only the birth of King David, but the birth of King Jesus. Notice even at this stage in the story the subtle hint so cleverly inserted by our author, that we are standing at a turning point for the nation: 'So Naomi returned from Moab accompanied by Ruth the Moabitess, her daughter-in-law, arriving in Bethlehem as the barley harvest was beginning' (1:22). So there is bread again in the house of bread; well, well, well. And when do they start reaping it? Just as Ruth arrives. What a coincidence!

A lesson about loving

We live in a world where human relationships are proving less than happy far too often. Erich Fromm in *The Sane Society* observes, 'There is not much love to be found in the world of today. There is rather a superficial friendliness concealing a distance, an indifference, a subtle distrust.' Karen Horney in *The Neurotic Personality of our Time* writes, 'The normal of our time feels comparatively isolated ... in the dilemma of hungering for a great deal of affection but finding difficulty in obtaining it.' Christopher Lasch writes in *The Culture of Narcissism*, 'Our society ... has made lasting friendships, love affairs and marriages increasingly difficult to achieve.' Social life has become more and more warlike. Personal relationships have taken on the nature of combat. Some dignify the combat by offering courses in assertiveness training, others celebrate the impermanent attachments that result with slogans like 'the open marriage'. But in so doing they merely intensify the dissatisfaction with the quality of human relationships that lies at the heart of our problem. Do phrases like 'superficial friendship', 'emotional isolation' and 'pervasive dissatisfaction with the quality of relationships' ring any bells with you? They certainly do with me. This is our world. It is no surprise that the statistics of rape are becoming worse, or that ethnic tension and domestic violence are growing the way they are. And is it any wonder that we find our own economy vulnerable to recession and instability? In a capitalist society, what is a sinking stock market, a turbulent exchange rate or chronic inflation but the modern equivalent of 'there was famine in the land?'

The reason for our economic problems, our crime rates and divorce statistics is not in our stars but in ourselves. We are not victims of fate. Such things are always the judicial chastening of God. There is no faithfulness, no covenant love, no acknowledgment of God in the land, and therefore the land mourns. The Bible says that that connection will be made in the experience of any society that flouts God's moral norms.

But the encouragement that the story of Ruth brings is that you and I can do something about it. We do not have to have a Cabinet post to do so; we do not have to walk the corridors of power to turn the tide for our society. What the book of Ruth has the audacity to suggest is that a single act of heroic love on the part of an insignificant, ethnically alien widow was the key to the whole of Israel's future blessing. That is why the world needs to see how we Christians love each other. There is nothing we can do for this sinsick world of ours more powerful than to demonstrate, like Ruth, the nature of God's covenant love in our dealings with one another.

This is a particularly poignant message for people who are single. Many struggle with that loneliness, and often resent it. Whether they're divorced, bereaved or have never married, deep down like Naomi they resent the way God has dealt with them. It's understandable; who wouldn't feel the same? But we do not have to wallow in self-pity, just as Naomi did not have to. There is an alternative response, a way out of bitterness into blessing. It requires great faith and sacrifice, but noble Ruth demonstrates that it is possible. She made singleness not her fate, but her choice. She committed herself, in covenant love, not to a husband but to a widow. Her wifely devotion and maternal energies, would be – at least for a period of time – sublimated in serving and caring for a lonely, vulnerable person in desperate need of support. She made that choice.

Do you have any idea how many such lonely and vulnerable and desperate Naomis there are in the world today? We desperately need Ruths who are prepared to sacrifice their own desires and fulfilment to reach out to them.

I think of a woman who has abandoned her career in order to care for an elderly relative with Alzheimer's disease – is that not covenant love?

I think of a man who I know has refused promotion in order to have more time to spend with his growing children – is that not covenant love?

I know a student who has surrendered his place in the Cambridge First Eleven in order to take a handicapped child to McDonald's every Saturday afternoon – is that not covenant love?

I think of a nurse who has accepted what will probably be lifelong singleness, as the price of her calling to care for AIDS victims in Uganda – is that not covenant love?

I think of a couple who have accepted their own childlessness as an opportunity to foster the orphaned, abused, hurting children of a Liverpool suburb – is that not covenant love?

I think of a person I know who in the pressures of an extremely busy and demanding life makes space to 'be there', reliably and instantly, for their friends whenever they are needed – is that not covenant love?

Don't let anybody tell you such things do not matter. Don't let anybody tell you such things do not count. We have it on the authority of our Master himself: 'If anyone gives even a cup of cold water to one of these little ones because he is my disciple, I tell you the truth, he will certainly not lose his reward' (Matthew 10:42). What you and I do in our world or personal relationships matters on a scale far beyond our own petty lives. What to the eyes of unbelief seems like a pointless sacrifice – a histrionic gesture, of no value or significance at all – may be in God's eyes a crucial event in his great cosmic plan.

Ruth leaves the security of her homeland in order to care for an embittered old lady. Christ leaves the glory of heaven to die lonely, upon a cross of wood.

A futile sacrifice? A histrionic gesture? No; upon such individual acts of moral heroism the very destiny of our world is hinged. That is the faith of the Christian. It's that insight which this story is trying to help us understand. It's not for nothing that Jesus tells us to take up our cross and follow him.

6

Love ...
Ruth 2 – 3

One day Naomi her mother-in-law said to her, 'My daughter, should I not try to find a home for you, where you will be well provided for? Is not Boaz, with whose servant girls you have been, a kinsman of ours? Tonight he will be winnowing barley on the thresh-ing-floor. Wash and perfume yourself, and put on your best clothes. Then go down to the threshing-floor, but don't let him know you are there until he has finished eating and drinking. When he lies down, note the place where he is lying. Then go and uncover his feet and lie down. He will tell you what to do.'

'I will do whatever you say,' Ruth answered. So she went down to the threshing-floor and did everything her mother-in-law told her to do.

When Boaz had finished eating and drinking and was in good spirits, he went over to lie down at the far end of the grain pile. Ruth approached quietly, uncovered his feet and lay down. In the middle of the night something startled the man, and he turned and discovered a woman lying at his feet.

'Who are you?' he asked.

'I am your servant Ruth,' she said. 'Spread the corner of your garment over me, since you are a kinsman-redeemer' (3:1–9).

Harry was going to church. He pulled out of his drive in his two-seater sports car, grateful that he had repaired the leak in the hood. It had been raining heavily since dawn and showed no sign of relenting. As he turned the corner into the main road, he saw ahead of him three figures huddled forlornly under a single umbrella beside the bus stop. They were all familiar because they all attended Harry's church. The first was old Mrs Fosdyke. She was well over seventy and suffered great pain from her rheumatism and arthritis, which he knew was always worse in damp weather. The second was Dr Roberts, the local GP. Harry as good as owed this man his life; a year before, he had diagnosed a rare and dangerous illness that Harry had contracted on holiday in the tropics, and had successfully treated it. The third in line was Julia. Harry had entertained a burning passion for Julia ever since she'd come to live in the area, though secretly, for as yet he'd found no opportunity to ask her out.

Harry glanced at the solitary passenger seat beside him. He had only a few seconds to make his decision, but it was enough. With an impressive screech of brakes he drew up at the bus stop. Magnanimously he presented the keys to Dr Roberts; attentively he lowered Mrs Fosdyke into the passenger seat. Then, with a modest wave, he bid them good-bye while he huddled close to Julia under the umbrella, praying earnestly that the number 8 bus would be even later than usual this Sunday.

The point of my story is this. In matters of romance, meeting the right person is almost invariably the result of a happy collusion between serendipity and science, good fortune and good sense; or, to use the vocabulary of a Christian theologian, it's the result of mysterious interaction between divine providence and human responsibility. God put Julia by the bus stop, but Harry had to work out how to get under the umbrella. It will often be like that. Indeed it is this co-operation between God's sovereign control of events and our personal initiative in exploiting opportunities that forms the necessary background, not just to a successful love life, but to the life of faith generally. And there are few more charming examples of that interplay than this story of Ruth.

Naomi has returned to Bethlehem in Judah in the wake of a disastrous domestic tragedy, and against her strong advice she is accompanied by Ruth. As we saw in the last chapter, Ruth's decision to accompany her was, humanly speaking, a crazy one: Judah was a dangerous place and Naomi was poverty-stricken. The plot of land Elimelech owned in Bethlehem hadn't been worked for at least ten years, and it would be six months at least before it would yield an income. In the meantime these women would have to survive by begging.

The toughest aspect of Ruth's decision was that it was ruinous for her marriage prospects. She was a foreigner, had no a dowry, and there was a question mark over her fertility, since in ten years of marriage she had born Naomi no grandchildren.

From every point of view, Ruth and Naomi looked set

145

to share their loneliness indefinitely. It was a bleak and insecure outlook, especially in the male-dominated and violent society in which they lived. Yet the story of Ruth, we know, has a happy ending. Against all the odds, Ruth will find a husband, and Naomi will become a grandmother. More startling even than that, the family line thus begun will in due course bring forth a royal dynasty, the dynasty of David and of God's Messiah, Jesus Christ.

So this is a classic rags-to-riches romance; the story of how Cinderella finds her prince and they live happily ever after. But notice in these central chapters how the inspired narrator quite deliberately draws our attention to the two concurrent influences that shape the outcome of his plot; divine providence and human responsibility. God puts Boaz by the bus stop, but Ruth must find a way to put herself under the umbrella.

God's providence

> May the LORD repay you for what you have done. May you be richly rewarded by the LORD, the God of Israel, under whose wings you have come to take refuge (2:12).

Right from the beginning of the story, our narrator has been quietly drawing our attention to the all-embracing nature of those providential, divine wings that are protecting Ruth. Remember, at the end of chapter 1, Naomi's self-pitying complaint about the cruel misfortune that had befallen her. She leaves us in no doubt that all this misery is down to God; it was his providence that appointed her sad lot. No less than four times in chapter

1 she directly affirms that it is the Lord, the Almighty, who is responsible for all that has gone wrong in her life. 'Don't call me Naomi ... Call me Mara, because the LORD has made my life very bitter. I went away full, but the LORD has brought me back empty ...The LORD has afflicted me; the Almighty has brought misfortune upon me' (1:20–21).

Who can blame her for that sense of betrayal and disappointment? First the austerity of the famine that drove them to Moab, then the loss of her husband, then the loss of her two sons; such a personal history isn't calculated to engender feelings of gratitude towards God. Yet, as readers of this story possessing the benefit of a bird's-eye view, and with our focus already on that happy ending that we know must be the final outcome, we know that all this was no chance chain of events. Ruth the Moabitess would never have come to Bethlehem, would never have known the God of Israel, would never have played the special part she would play in the family tree of King David and Jesus, were it not for all that misfortune that befell Naomi. Naomi's theology was not at fault. God's providence was indeed supervising the cruel tragedy of her life. But what she felt (at least in the early stages) to be arbitrary strokes of some sadistic heavenly tyrant were, if only she had known it, necessary preparatory moves in a cosmic plan of salvation so mind-blowing and so grand in its conception, that it would have defeated even the imagination of our sacred author. In the words of William Cowper's great hymn, 'God moves in a mysterious way, His wonders to perform.'

> Judge not the LORD by feeble sense,
> But trust him for his grace;

Behind a frowning providence,
He hides a smiling face.

In fact, God's providential ways in chapter 1 are even more mysterious than Naomi gives him credit for. As we have seen, the story begins with what any informed Jewish reader would have regarded as a lamentable error of human judgment. Elimelech, Naomi's husband, under the economic pressure of the famine, chooses to emigrate to Moab – an enemy nation of idolaters about which there were explicit warnings in the law of Moses. No pious Jew would have made such a choice.

And yet, extraordinarily, if Elimelech had not made that choice, the story of Ruth would never have got beyond 1:1. There is comfort, surely, in such observations! Many of us torture ourselves with vain regrets. 'If only I hadn't made that mistake,' we say. 'I forfeited God's purpose for me by that early act of folly.'

But it is nonsense. Where in the Bible do human mistakes ever obstruct his purpose? Nowhere. On the contrary, the Bible constantly testifies to how God, by master strokes of consummate skill, achieves his purposes precisely by means of our human mistakes. What was Judas's betrayal of the Master, if it was not a mistake? Yet without that mistake, Christ would not have saved the world. So don't allow past mistakes to haunt you. Mistakes though they were, and regrettable ones, God has used them. The bud may have a bitter taste, as Naomi found. But trust him; the flower will be sweet when it blooms.

A hidden hand

Follow this story through the next two chapters, and you will see how this divine providence that had so savagely devastated Naomi's life was all the time actually working things out; not only for her good, but for the good of Ruth her daughter-in-law, and for the people of God as a whole. Early in chapter 2 our author drops a couple of gentle hints into his narrative that are designed to sensitize us to this underlying divine directedness in the whole affair. As we have seen throughout this book, in Old Testament narrative it is the gentle hints that you have to pick up, if you are to identify the author's purpose.

In 2:1, for instance, he tells us, 'Now Naomi had a relative on her husband's side from the clan of Elimelech, a man of standing, whose name was Boaz.' Why mention that? Arguably he has deprived himself of a very useful dramatic device by telling us about Boaz's affiliation to Naomi's dead husband so early in the story. If he'd held the information back, he could have held us in greater suspense and generated a much more climactic dénouement when the identity of Boaz was revealed.

But that criticism fails to recognize our author's motivation. He is a very skilled storyteller, but he is willing to sacrifice dramatic impact if necessary in order to achieve his theological purpose. He wants us to have an insight into the divine providence, a divine providence of which Ruth herself, at this point in the story, was necessarily unaware. The man of Ruth's dreams is there, waiting in the wings like Julia by the bus stop.

Later, in chapter 2, Ruth goes out to glean the loose grains of barley that have fallen in the field behind the harvesters. The poor were allowed to do this in Israel; it was neither trespass nor theft, though it seems to have been a courtesy to ask permission before you did it. Whose field does she 'just happen' to select for her gleaning activity? The field of Boaz. She doesn't know him, she's never seen him. Only we, the readers, have this privileged information about who he was. She has absolutely no idea of his future significance in her life. The Hebrew of 2:3 emphasizes this: 'By chance [NIV 'As it turned out'] she found herself working in the field belonging to Boaz.' Of course we know that it was not chance. Why? Because our author has alerted us to Boaz's identity. We detect the hidden hand of providence at work. And as if to confirm our suspicions, who shows up at midday to see how things are going? The man himself. In verse 4 the Hebrew says, 'Behold' (NIV 'Just then'). It is an interjection of surprise and wonder. Once again our author wants to alert us to divine providence at work.

The romance begins

Humanly speaking, it is a fortuitous encounter. Two pairs of eyes meet for the first time across a harvest field on a summer's day. On the one hand, a penniless widow doing her best to retain her dignity and pay her bills, but forced by circumstances to do the ancient equivalent of rifling dustbins; on the other, a handsome hero, considerably older than her but, as our author puts it, a man of standing in the community. And to judge from his pious greeting to the workers on his land, a man of faith, too.

Our imaginations are already racing ahead in anticipation of where this meeting may lead, for it's quite clear God has a hand in it. This is not mere chance, and when Ruth gets home and tells Naomi how this strange man had treated her so nicely, Naomi knew it wasn't chance too!

> Her mother-in-law asked her, 'Where did you glean today? Where did you work? Blessed be the man who took notice of you!'
> Then Ruth told her mother-in-law about the one at whose place she had been working. 'The name of the man I worked with today is Boaz,' she said.
> 'The LORD bless him!' Naomi said to her daughter-in-law. 'He has not stopped showing his kindness to the living and the dead.' She added, 'That man is our close relative; he is one of our kinsman-redeemers' (2:19–20).

For the first time since her bereavement, Naomi's faith bursts into new life. God has given her a sign, albeit no larger than a cloud the size of a man's hand at this point in the story, but enough to restore her confidence in the trustworthiness of his goodness.

Sometimes, under the batterings of circumstance, our faith does ebb so low that we need some kind of evidential sign to reassure us. Like doubting Thomas, our cherished hopes are so brutally crucified that we must see the print of the nails before we will take the emotional risk of believing again. In Thomas's as in Naomi's case, God has mercy on such doubts. That is not to say that there is not a better path, of course. 'Because you have seen me, you have believed,' said the Master in gentle rebuke. 'Blessed are those who have not seen and yet have believed' (John 20:29). That was Ruth's blessing. She had seen nothing. She knew nothing. She had no sign. And yet throughout this story, her faith had not collapsed.

She'd forsaken the idolatrous culture of her homeland and entered a solemn covenant with Naomi and Naomi's God, in spite of the fact that God had done absolutely nothing for her up to this point. 'May you be richly rewarded by the LORD, the God of Israel, under whose wings you have come to take refuge,' prays noble Boaz. Well, indeed she will, Boaz. And in the sovereign providence of God, you will have a lot more to do with it than you realize right now ... Which brings us to the other side of the story.

Human responsibility

> 'Who are you?' he asked.
> 'I am your servant Ruth,' she said, 'Spread the corner of your garment over me, since you are a kinsman-redeemer' (3:9).

A number of recent commentators have drawn attention to the relevance of the story of Ruth to the feminist debate. It's not difficult to see why; Ruth is quite an audacious lady. She doesn't need a man to tell her what to do. Indeed, contrary to all the cultural expectations of ancient patriarchal society, she comes close to telling Boaz what to do. This is no shrinking violet who is content to simper in the background in the expectation that God will drop his blessings in her lap. Ruth is the kind of woman who will, as far as she can, by her own enterprise and energy, work for the fulfilment of God's purpose in her life. We saw the first sign of that individual strength of character in her heroic commitment to Naomi. We see it again in chapter 2 in her diligent application to the task of gleaning. Naomi seems to have been either too demoralized by her grief or too humiliated by her reduced circumstances to go out and gather corn like a pauper. But Ruth suffers no such paralysis. She's not a woman to sit at home and wallow in self-pity or wounded pride. She had trusted God that he still had a future for her. She didn't know what it was, but while she waited for further light on that score, she was determined to make a living for herself and her mother-in-law.

Significantly, it is while she is engaged in the process of getting on with the business of living that God brings to her attention the husband he has in mind for her. Throughout this story, God's favour is only experienced by men and women as they are active in faith. Nobody finds blessing in this tale by doing nothing. We know that at this point, Ruth has no more idea than Boaz has of what is to come. She is, perhaps, just a little flattered by the attention of this older, wealthier man. But there has been nothing in the least flirtatious about Boaz's behaviour. On the contrary, his chief concern was to prevent her suffering any kind of sexual harassment from the workers. His attitude throughout is more that of a benefactor than that of a would-be lover.

Was he a widower himself? It's possible, certainly. His comment in 3:10, 'The LORD bless you, my daughter ... This kindness is greater than that which you showed earlier: You have not run after the younger men, whether rich or poor,' seems to indicate that he thought he was so far into mid-life that marriage was no longer on the cards for him. There were too many good-looking younger rivals around. Perhaps he felt that to court a bride at his age and in his social position would have seemed undignified; an invitation to humiliation and mockery that a

153

person of his social standing shouldn't risk. He certainly entertained no serious anticipation of any romantic liaison between him and this Moabite woman.

But he was nevertheless attracted to her. That much is obvious. Our narrator is keen to stress also that it wasn't a simple physical attraction either. It was her character that had impressed him; he draws attention to it. He'd noticed her hard work in the fields. Everybody had noticed her sacrificial commitment to Naomi. And most of all, he was impressed by her faith in the God of Israel, a faith which was all the more obvious in its genuineness because she was a foreigner.

Boaz knew, of course, the negative things which the law of Moses said about Moab, but he was a sufficiently spiritual man to realize that it was no part of God's intention to sanctify racism by that law. What was wrong with Moab was its idolatry and its hostility to the people of God. When a Moabite woman abandoned that idolatry and hostility, she was every bit as entitled to seek refuge under the wings of Jehovah as any Jew was. I'm sure there were plenty of others in Bethlehem who would not have looked at things that way; they would have looked at Ruth with far more xenophobic prejudice. But Boaz, to his credit, did not. Instead he assured Ruth that she had his personal support. 'May I continue to find favour in your eyes, my lord,' she says in 2:13. 'You have given me comfort and have spoken kindly to your servant – though I do not have the standing of one of your servant girls.'

It is not difficult to imagine how Ruth's eyes brighten as she speaks those words. A man has noticed her. A noble and a good man has treated her with respect, not just as a 'bit of all right' to laugh about with his male friends later on in the day. One wonders; had she ever been treated

154

that way before? Who could blame her for finding such attention igniting a little flame of romance in her heart?

As we have seen, Ruth understood covenant love, love that involved commitment and sacrifice. She knew that was the kind of love that the God of Israel demonstrated himself and expected his people to demonstrate in their relationships with each other. And here at last she sensed that, in that often godless Israel in the time of the judges, she had met a man who shared her convictions and her understanding on that matter. Naomi also agreed. See how she responds: 'My daughter, should I not try to find a home for you, where you will be well provided for? Is not Boaz, with whose servant girls you have been, a kinsman of ours?' (3:1–2). Yes, God's providence has pointed the way; but the time for passive waiting is passed. An active step of personal initiative is now required.

Ruth takes matters into her own hands

Boaz had no idea that Ruth considered him an eligible prospect. How could she let him know? It was going to be far from easy, given the constraints of oriental sexual protocol. She would have to choose the right place and the right time. But with Naomi's wise counsel to guide her, she chose well; one senses our narrator has his tongue firmly in his cheek, as he recounts in the early verses of chapter 3 this conspiracy of feminine wiles.

First, the beauty treatment. 'I think a little splash of Chanel No. 5 wouldn't go amiss tonight, my dear,' says Naomi. 'And what about that nice little black number you look so nice in?' Then, the right moment; 'Well,' says Naomi, 'night-time is so much more romantic than the day, don't you think? And you need to catch him in a nice relaxed mood. Go down to the threshing floor, but don't let him know you're there until he's finished eating and drinking. When he lies down, note the place where he is lying. Then go and uncover his feet and lie down. He will tell you what to do.'

One gets the distinct impression that Naomi was an old hand at this kind of thing!

There is considerable debate among commentators about the significance of the phrase 'uncovering the feet'. The more modest suggest that the purpose here is simply to wake Boaz gently when he feels his toes are getting cold. But it does have to be said that in the ancient world the word 'feet' was sometimes used in Hebrew as a euphemism for the genitals. So some commentators interpret according to that reading. At the very least, we have to say, this action which Ruth took was decidedly *risqué*. By approaching a man in the pitch dark she was gambling not just with her dignity, but also with her chastity. If he chose to take sexual advantage of the situation, she would have no defence. What on earth was she doing uncovering a man at that time of night? Everybody knew what sort of hanky-panky people got up to after the harvest thanksgiving party. Had she read the nobility of this man's character correctly? Would he understand her motives properly? It was all a huge risk. Our hearts are in our mouths as this situation unfolds.

But sometimes life demands such risks. It isn't always enough simply to wait passively on God's providence. Sometimes we have to take responsibility for our destiny. Sometimes we have to exercise our God-given power of self-determination. A courageous, enterprising, even opportunistic, initiative is sometimes required of us if we are not to forfeit the blessings that God is only too willing to bestow. And Ruth, this woman of character, displays that initiative here.

Naomi, you notice, had advised her to keep her mouth shut and let Boaz do all the talking. But rather charmingly, Ruth is far too irrepressible for such reticence. '"Who are you?" he asked. "I am your servant Ruth," she said, "Spread the corner of your garment over me, since you are a kinsman-redeemer."'

This is an instance where it really does help to know a little bit of Hebrew, because the phrase, 'Spread the corner of your garment over me' is deliciously ambiguous. On the one hand it is regularly used in Semitic culture as a euphemism for marriage. 'Spread the corner of your garment over me' means 'marry me'. But on the other hand the Hebrew word for garment, or skirt, in 3:9 is actually the same plural word that was translated back in 2:12 as 'wings'. 'Spread your wings on me' invites Ruth. I have no doubt at all that our author quite deliberately intends an echo of those earlier words of Boaz.

Do you see what Ruth is saying? 'You prayed for my blessing, Boaz, since I had sought the protective wings of Jehovah. Well now, Boaz, let's face it, you're my dead husband's kinsman, one of the few he had. Isn't it up to you to do more than pray for me? Isn't it your responsibility, under God's covenant law, to redeem me from my helplessness as a widow? Don't you see, Boaz, that you are the answer to your own prayer? The protective wings of Jehovah are *your* wings. Spread them over me, then. Marry me.'

She's an audacious lady indeed! And, as we shall see, marry her he does.

The passivity and activity of faith

Learn, then, from this story of Ruth that faith is at once passive and active. It's passive in the sense that faith must sometimes be content to wait for God to act: 'Be still before the LORD and wait patiently for him,' says the psalmist. For it is he, ultimately, who organizes the circumstances of our life. '[He] works out everything', says the apostle, 'in conformity with the purpose of his will' (Ephesians 1:11). Faith means trusting that divine purpose, trusting that it is a loving purpose, even when we cannot feel the love; trusting him that it is a purpose that can be relied upon to work all things together for our good. We see that faith in Ruth, as she accepts her tragic and bereaved situation with good grace, refusing, unlike Naomi perhaps, to let resentment fester in her heart. Faith in this respect is the opposite of fretful anxiety. It is patience, contentment, even resignation.

But that does not mean that faith is complacency, idleness or negligence. There's all the difference in the world between trusting in God and twiddling your thumbs. For faith also demands action, enterprise, endeavour. God appoints means by which we receive his grace and he expects us to employ those means when we have opportunity. 'By faith Abraham, when called to go to a place he would later receive as his inheritance, obeyed and went, even though he did not know where he was going' (Hebrews 11:8), comments the author of Hebrews. In doing so Abraham becomes the paradigm of that spirit of adventure which characterizes biblical faith. Faith sometimes requires us to take risks. Calculated risks, it's true; the believer isn't a frivolous dare-devil who hazards his or her life in wanton recklessness. Faith assesses the risks it takes. Its audacity is measured and thoughtful. But to unbelieving eyes it may sometimes seem as if faith means playing Russian roulette with fate.

Ruth's audacious words to Boaz here are a case in point. What Jewish male could fail to be offended by such a reversal of roles? It was the man who did the proposing, not the woman – most certainly so in those days, even if not today. But such a convention would have left the two of them locked for ever in the tragic irony of their unfulfilled happiness. Ruth had to take the initiative in the relationship, for Boaz was too self-deprecating even to consider the possibility that a young woman like Ruth might want him. I say again, Ruth is a lesson to us, not only in that passive waiting on God, but also in that active, launching out upon God. She illustrates the tension between the patience of faith and the gamble of faith.

There is an anonymous prayer that is often quoted: 'Give me, good Lord, the grace to perform with diligence those things I can do; to accept with humility those things I cannot do; and the wisdom to distinguish between the two.' People become unbalanced in their lives, as often as not because they lack that wisdom. On one hand, some people tend to become apathetic fatalists, convinced that nothing can possibly make any difference to the way things will work out. Like Omar Khayyam, they resign themselves to fate and see God as a divine chess-player:

'Tis all a chequer-board of nights and days
Where Destiny with Men for pieces plays ...

On the other hand, some people become over-confident egoists, sure that they can manufacture their own happiness, boasting like the poet W. E. Henley:

In the fell clutch of circumstance
I have not winced nor cried aloud ...
I am the master of my fate:
I am the captain of my soul.

The path of faith lies in neither of those extremes; it understands, and reckons on, both divine providence and human responsibility. Behind the sometimes mysterious and paradoxical interaction of these two fundamental truths of our existence lies God's desire to make a world, over which he is the undeniable sovereign but in which we also enjoy meaningful freedom. We are not disposable pawns on his chess board; we are not puppets manipulated by hidden strings; we are voluntary agents able to make real and responsible choices. Yet we are not the masters of our fate either. Our liberty is constrained within the circle of his permission and his loving oversight. Only a God as all-knowing and as all-mighty as he is could work such a miracle. It is not surprising if we, with our much more limited understanding and powers, are bewildered about how these two things can both be true without one being sacrificed to the other. But the Bible insists it is so. God chooses to work his sovereign will by means of our free decisions, and he has built our free decisions, good and bad, into his cosmic plan.

Think about prayer. How does it work? God knows what he's going to do. He reads the future with infallible precision. So how can prayer change anything? It changes things only because God has chosen to work out his will through our prayers. He is determined to involve us in his purposes, and prayer is one of the major ways he achieves that goal. So we are not passive, ignorant pawns, but active and intelligent collaborators with his purpose.

Think about our Christian growth in holiness. How does that happen? The Bible says that God conforms us to the likeness of his Son (Romans 8:29). Yet you and I know that that process of moral change does not take place except by our voluntary decision to live in ways that please him. The Holy Spirit is not a spiritual rapist. He waits upon our willingness.

Think about the business of gaining our daily bread. Jesus told his disciples, 'Look at the birds of the air; they do not sow or reap or store away in barns, and yet your heavenly Father feeds them. Are you not much more valuable than they?' (Matthew 6:26). In other words, he is saying, 'Trust the loving providence of God to meet your material needs.' But does that mean that we are to sit with our hands folded, waiting for God to put the food in our mouths? Suppose some superspiritual little bird of the air were to take that line and decide he was not going to go out to look for worms this morning but was going to sit in his nest and live by faith. That pious little fowl would quickly starve to death for lack of faith – a faith that uses the freedom with which God has endowed it, to hunt those worms that he has provided.

Think about the issue of guidance, and particularly in the context of Ruth. Some of you may be single and would like to find a marital partner. Let the story of Ruth teach you patience; wait for God in his providence to put the right person by the bus stop. But let it teach you also the appropriateness of decision and initiative: when opportunity presents itself, be ready to put yourself under the umbrella.

Don't be mistaken. It is not the case that God's providence contributes fifty per cent of events and we are left to make up the other fifty per cent. God's providence is at work all the time. He's overruling our clumsy efforts to get under the umbrella, just as he overruled the lateness of the bus. But sometimes his acts in providence leave us with nothing to do, whereas at other times his acts of providence require from us an active initiative, a considered step of faith.

Think about salvation itself. The Bible says that every saved soul was predestined before the foundation of the world (Ephesians 1:4). Yet how does that divine purpose find fulfilment? It finds fulfilment as we actively repent and believe. God does not repent and believe for us. We do it. A decision is required of us.

Think about the cross; where, the Bible tells us, the Son of God died in a way that was planned in the eternal counsels of God before the world was made. Yet what do we see in Gethsemane? We see a self-determining man, wrestling in prayer and saying, 'Not my will, but your will be done.' Was the will of God in doubt? Was Jesus just a pawn in the divine purpose? Was Gethsemane just a huge theatrical sham? Certainly not. God has so woven the rich tapestry of his purpose together that eternity is contingent on history. The fate of the universe is different because that man, that free man, on that Passover night, chose to grasp the wood of a Roman gibbet which he could very easily have avoided. 'Not my will, but yours be done.' He went to that cross as a voluntary sacrifice. It was God's will, but it was also his choice. And there above all, perhaps, we see the mysterious way in which the divine providential ruling of events intersects with human responsibility. We see how the jigsaw puzzle of human destiny is resolved by these twin forces.

So do not be paralysed by morbid fatalism. But do not

be driven, either, by anxious self-reliance. Live, like Ruth, a life of patience and enterprise. In other words, live by faith.

7

... and marriage
Ruth 4

So Boaz took Ruth and she became his wife. Then he
went to her, and the LORD enabled her to conceive,
and she gave birth to a son. The women said to
Naomi: 'Praise be to the LORD, who this day has not
left you without a kinsman-redeemer. May he
become famous throughout Israel! He will renew
your life and sustain you in your old age. For your
daughter-in-law, who loves you and who is better to
you than seven sons, has given him birth.'

Then Naomi took the child, laid him in her lap
and cared for him. The women living there said,
'Naomi has a son.' And they named him Obed. He
was the father of Jesse, the father of David (4:13–17).

Few cultures have bandied the word 'love' around more
freely than has ours. Yet an enormous number of people
do experience great difficulty in finding the quality of

interpersonal relationship they really want in love. All too often love proves elusive, and empty sex takes its place.

Erich Fromm in his book *The Act of Loving* blames it all on the economic system. It's capitalism, he says, that has rendered real love impossible by its cultivation of self-interest. Men and women do not really love one another any more, they use one another for the fulfilment of their individual needs. It's a kind of commercial contract. Just as a car owner uses a mechanic to service his car, so men and women use each other.

Other sociologists have drawn attention to the role which the eroticization of society by the media has played. Forty years ago, the publication of D. H. Lawrence's novel *Lady Chatterley's Lover* was scandalous enough to merit a High Court action under the Obscene Publications Act. Now we have soft pornography, thinly disguised as sex education videos, on sale in High Street supermarkets. We have girlie magazines that would once have been available only in some curtained dive in Soho, now freely available at the newsagent on the corner. Advertisers seem incapable of marketing even so mundane a commodity as a bar of chocolate without turning it into some object of phallic fantasy. Expectations of sexual athleticism in one's partner, and of sexual ecstasy in oneself, have been raised to dizzying heights by this onslaught of eroticism. I suspect that never since the days of the Roman Empire has the general level of sexual arousal in society been so high. And in such a world it isn't surprising if the distinction between love and lust gets rather blurred. To quote the poet Steve Turner, instead of 'making' love, we end up 'faking' it.

Habits of the heart

Is capitalism to blame for this proliferation of shallow relationships? Or is the culprit the sex-mad media? A sociological study that sheds an enormous amount of light on the question was published in the 1980s. Entitled *The Habits of the Heart*, it was produced by a small group of sociologists at Berkeley University in California, and analyses people's attitudes towards social commitments. The theme of the whole study is the tension between individual freedom and social commitment. One of its most significant findings concerned people's attitudes towards feelings. What the compilers discovered was that people with traditional ideas took the view that feelings should always be subordinated to duty. Hence they placed a high value on such virtues as self-control, self-denial, self-discipline, self-sacrifice. They saw marital love as a commitment of the will, to be honoured irrespective of whether one's feelings about it were good or bad.

But the research revealed that the traditional attitude was very rapidly being displaced in modern society by a different attitude, which they called the 'therapeutic' attitude. On this view, feelings take priority over everything else. The important virtues are not those that restrain the expression of the self, but those which liberate it. Honesty and openness are what count, not self-discipline, self-denial, self-control or self-sacrifice; but rather self-fulfilment, self-realization, self-acceptance, self-actualization. These are the buzz words of the therapeutic attitude. The therapeutic ideal of love is spontaneous sharing of feelings between authentic, expressive individuals, and long-term commitment does not necessarily feature in such a relationship at all. According to this atti-

166

tude, if my emotional needs are not being met by my partner I am entitled to sever the relationship.

The therapeutic attitude denies all forms of social obligation or duty, replacing them with the ideals of open and honest communication. The only thing a therapeutically liberated lover owes to his or her partner is to share his or her feelings fully. Emotional independence and self-sufficiency are the goal. A personal relationship is simply seen as a device for achieving this essentially individualistic goal.

I am not saying that the therapeutic attitude is all bad. Undoubtedly it does do some people a great service, by helping them to get in touch with their own wants and needs and emancipating them from the artificial constraints of cramping social roles and guilt-inducing manipulations by other people. I have seen enough in pastoral situations to recognize that making a martyr of oneself is not always the right and Christian thing to do.

But it has to be said that this kind of therapeutic attitude, carried to an extreme, is desperately corrosive of loving relationships. No doubt capitalism, by its endorsement of self-interest, has prepared the ground for such a new attitude, and no doubt the media in its preoccupation with erotic images has encouraged and exploited it. But the root of our twentieth-century decay in loving interpersonal relationships between the sexes is not economic or erotic. It is moral. In the past half-century we have changed the goalposts. We have redefined the meaning of the word 'love'. It is no longer a sacrificial commitment to another person; love is now an intensity of feeling within myself. That change has come about very subtly, but it is now, I think, universal.

Committed love

The book of Ruth is all about the difference that inter-personal commitment can make to our experience of the meaning of love. It's possible, argues this book, to redis-cover that blend of intimacy and security that only real, committed love can provide. The book of Ruth encour-ages us to believe in that love, old-fashioned though it may seem.

The time of the judges in which this book is set was another period when the old moral order was disintegrat-ing. Everybody did what they wanted to do. A thoroughly individualistic hedonistic society was developing, with the result that sexual brutality and criminal violence were commonplace. But Ruth, like a candle in the darkness, offers us a touching beacon of hope in that very society where the law of the jungle generally prevailed. I suspect that even in its own time the book of Ruth was an old-fashioned book. It is a classic historical romance; it offers its reader an affirmation of the old traditional values of love. Yet there's nothing sentimental about the story. It is meant to convince us that love defined as a sacrificial commitment to somebody else is the toughest and noblest kind of love. It's about loyalty and duty, and the cost that loyalty and duty impose. It's about putting the needs of other people above our own. It's about how God achieves his purposes in history through insignificant little people, who trust him enough to take the risks which such sacri-ficial committed love demands.

We saw the first example of this kind of love, you remember, in chapter 1. Ruth, contrary to all good sense and against her own best interests, commits herself in love to her widowed mother-in-law Naomi. Rather than leave this older woman bereft, Ruth abandons her own country of Moab and accompanies Naomi to Judah. 'Where you go I will go, and where you stay I will stay. Your people will be my people and your God my God.' She deliberately echoes the covenant vow of Jehovah to Israel in her covenant vow to Naomi.

Such a covenant relationship is what real love is all about. If Ruth had only been interested in her own self-fulfilment she would have ditched Naomi and gone in search of a husband from among her own people. But she was part of Naomi's family, one of the few members of that family left alive, and she was determined to put that loyalty first.

As if to reinforce that same lesson, at the end of the book our author presents us with a second example. This time, though Ruth is the catalyst, somebody else demonstrates the demands of such committed covenant love: Boaz.

The law's provision for widows

To make sense of these last two chapters of Ruth we need to learn a little about the legal provisions that Old Testament law made for widows. There were two particularly relevant pieces of legislation.

The first was *the law of levirate marriage*. It is explained in Deuteronomy 25 that there was an obligation on the part of a dead man's brother to take his brother's widow into his own household. If she had no children, he was further obligated to marry her and to have a child by her, so that his brother would have an heir to inherit that deceased brother's estate.

Today this might well seem a bizarre arrangement. But

it did solve an immensely important social problem: whose responsibility was it to care for a widow? The law of levirate marriage said that the responsibility fell, not on the widow's parental, but on her marital family and in particular on her brother-in-law.

The second piece of legislation which is relevant to this whole question of caring for widows and the book of Ruth, is *the law of redemption*, which is discussed in detail in Leviticus 25. This dealt not just with widows, but with any family member who fell on hard times. Perhaps they had fallen into debt and had to sell their family land; perhaps the debt was so large that they had had to sell themselves into slavery, too. In such a situation, the law said that a family member must take upon themself the role of 'kinsman-redeemer'. This is a technical term in Hebrew. The kinsman-redeemer should pay off the person's debts, redeeming both their property and their freedom.

If the law of levirate marriage seems bizarre to us, I suspect that the law of redemption must seem extraordinarily generous. Redemption could involve a very considerable sum of money. Could the law really require someone's relative to pay out such a huge sum for the sake of a relative who had fallen on hard times?

But it is precisely because the Old Testament sees love primarily as a moral commitment to another person, rather than a sentimental feeling, that it could require such acts of personal sacrifice. A man owed such sacrificial loyalty to his family. The law did not allow him to think in our modern categories of self-centred individualism. It cultivated mutual commitment by its very institutions.

What did these two pieces of ancient legislation mean for Ruth and her mother-in-law Naomi? As far as they could tell on their return to Judah, not very much. After all, obedience to the costly covenant law of Moses was presumably rare in the days of the judges. 'Do others before they do you,' was the popular philosophy of the streets. Widows probably stood more chance of being raped than redeemed in that lawless society. But more than that, Naomi's domestic tragedy had been so severe that it had left her with no close male relatives anyway, who could fulfil the moral obligation towards her which these laws required. Her daughter-in-law was in an even weaker position. One's responsibility to do something for an impoverished widow diminished as one's distance from kinship increased. A brother-in-law was required by law to do something for the widow of his dead brother – but it was unreasonable and unrealistic to expect distant relatives to feel the same degree of moral obligation.

So far as Naomi knew, distant relatives were all she had. The description of Boaz in 2:20 as a 'close relative' is a misleading translation in this respect, for the Hebrew simply implies that he was the *next* relative, or as it turns out, the next-but-one. In other words, he was one of the nearest relatives she had. But that does not necessarily imply that he was anything nearer than a second cousin twice removed. Indeed, the whole point of chapters 3 and 4 of this story (and on this the plot hinges) is that Boaz was so distant a relative that any action on his part was purely voluntary. There was no social expectation upon him to intervene in Naomi's affairs at all.

Yet he did. That is precisely what Ruth's urgent appeal to him in 3:9 is all about. 'Spread the corner of your garment over me ...' Why this euphemistic proposal of marriage? '... since you are a kinsman-redeemer'. In other words, 'I am a widow. The law says my brother-in-law should marry me and deliver me from the helplessness and hopelessness of my position in this male-dominated society. But I haven't got a brother-in-law, Boaz. I can only then appeal to you, as one of the nearest relatives I've got, to assume this role of kinsman-redeemer for me. Spread the corner of your garment over me. Marry me.'

As we have already observed, this was a phenomenally risky initiative on Ruth's part. She was gambling not just with her pride but with her virtue. Many a man would have told her to get lost. Worse still, many a man would have taken sexual advantage of her in this situation. But Boaz, as our author has already told us, was a gentleman. And it's quite clear he recognized a similar moral calibre in Ruth. See how he goes on:

> 'The LORD bless you, my daughter,' he replied. 'This kindness is greater than that which you showed earlier: You have not run after the younger men, whether rich or poor. And now, my daughter, don't be afraid. I will do for you all you ask. All my fellow townsmen know that you are a woman of noble character. Although it is true that I am near of kin, there is a kinsman-redeemer nearer than I. Stay here for the night, and in the morning if he wants to redeem, good; let him redeem. But if he is not willing, as surely as the LORD lives I will do it. Lie here until morning' (3:10–13).

It's important to understand the import of these words. Many a young widow in Ruth's position would have 'run after younger men'. She had no dowry to offer, and she was a foreigner. Both those things counted very seriously against her in the marriage stakes. But she was clearly attractive and shrewd, so she could easily have frequented the ancient equivalent of a singles bar and sought to entice some oversexed young man, who had little experience but plenty of cash, into a compromising situation from which the only escape would be matrimony. Such things happen today; you can be sure they happened then. Many a young woman in Ruth's situation would have felt compelled to use such unscrupulous tactics to secure her future.

But Ruth had not done so, commonly expected though such behaviour clearly was. She might thereby have secured a very comfortable position for herself; but if she had, then – quite apart from the moral implications – it would have left Naomi high and dry; any young gigolo she found that way would have no responsibility at all towards Naomi. So instead, true to the commitment she had made, Ruth refused to desert her mother-in-law and look for some young man of her own. Instead, she deliberately offered herself to Boaz, a man whom we know was old enough to be her father but was a potential kinsman-redeemer. If he assumed that legal responsibility, then both Ruth and Naomi's future would be secured.

That is what Boaz means when he says, 'This kindness is greater than that which you showed earlier.' He is referring to her kindness not to himself but to Naomi. He is acknowledging that the relationship that Ruth is offering him is, in part at any rate, a consequence of the loyal love she has pledged to his cousin Elimelech's widow. And he is a wise and humble enough man to recognize that a woman who understands love in that sacrificial and committed way is going to make a most outstanding wife. Ruth is indeed a woman of noble character. The community of Bethlehem had already begun to recognize that fact. But Boaz is confident they haven't yet seen the half of it.

Legal obstacle

The story is not yet over, however. There is a legal predicament to be overcome, and it could still torpedo that happy ending. For the role of kinsman-redeemer followed a strict order of precedence and Boaz, we discover now, was only second in line. It would take some delicate negotiations to oust his predecessor without having to offer any sweeteners. On no account must word get out that Boaz is actually attracted to Ruth and wants to marry her; if his rival were to sense some romantic interest in the matter, he would be sure to exploit the situation to his own financial advantage. Their meeting must be kept secret: 'So she lay at his feet until morning, but got up before anyone could be recognised; and he said, "Don't let it be known that a woman came to the threshing-floor"' (3:14).

Some commentators insist that Boaz's invitation to Ruth to stay the night must imply that sexual intercourse took place between them. But it seems to me that the text goes out of its way to insist that no such union took place. 'She lay at his feet,' we're told. It is, as we have seen, an expression that could be interpreted in more than one way, and it certainly implies some measure of physical intimacy. But I can find no Old Testament use of the phrase that implies any kind of actual sexual activity.

He tells her to wait till dawn, undoubtedly because there is danger involved in a young woman being out alone in the darkness. Because the matter must be kept secret, he cannot accompany her back to her home. Yet

Boaz is not yet Ruth's husband, and indeed, it may yet prove impossible for him to become her husband. There is no way he would risk her honour, or his own, by a foolish act of impatience.

There is an opportunity here, perhaps, for young couples to ponder on the necessary discretion of premarital life. No matter how sure you are about your intention to marry, things can and sometimes do go wrong. Engagements do break. So the path of prudence is to do as Boaz and Ruth did: make the covenant legal and public before you seal it irrevocably in physical union. Of course, there will be moments of private intimacy, of great tenderness, in that premarital period, but if we are wise, like Boaz, we will wait till the second ring is on the finger.

At the end of chapter 3 our author is holding us in suspense. Everybody else in Bethlehem is asleep, but Naomi isn't. 'When Ruth came to her mother-in-law, Naomi asked, "How did it go, my daughter?"' (3:16). The Hebrew means literally, 'Who are you?' – as if to say, 'Are you Mrs Boaz yet or not?' And on receiving Ruth's report, she, with us, waits with bated breath to see how Boaz is going to engineer the necessary legal coup to make a marriage to Ruth possible.

Problems solved

Boaz does not disappoint us. A carefully planned but apparently accidental meeting with the other relative in question provides him with the opportunity he needs for a public hearing of the case before the elders (4:1-12). What this poor man thinks is going to be a little private tête-à-tête suddenly turns into a major court case with all the clan-elders surrounding him. Wisely, Boaz doesn't mention Ruth at all. He treats it as only a question of property. Elimelech had held title to some land; by Israelite law that land passed to the next of kin, which was this unnamed relative. However, there was Naomi to consider. Any relative who took possession of Elimelech's land would be morally bound to provide for the widow too. It's in that sense, I suspect, that Boaz speaks of Naomi 'selling' the land, not that the freehold was hers to dispose of, because by Israelite law it wasn't; but in the sense that any kinsman that wanted to claim that land would have to agree to a financial settlement that would provide for her needs, or he would forfeit his claim to the land.

The kinsman at first considers this a bargain, because Naomi is, after all, old and she has no children. 'I will redeem it' (4:4), he says. The financial needs of Naomi would be few, and the property in question would make a nice addition to his estate. But then Boaz drops his bombshell: 'On the day you buy the land from Naomi and from Ruth the Moabitess, you acquire the dead man's widow, in order to maintain the name of the dead with his property' (4:5). In other words, Boaz is saying that there are two laws to consider here, not just one. 'If you're going to fulfil the role of kinsman-redeemer regarding Elimelech's property, you surely must take on board the legal responsibility of levirate marriage too, and according to that law you are duty-bound to raise up an heir to Elimelech; and though Naomi may be past child-bearing age, the widow of Elimelech's son is not,' argues Boaz before the elders. 'So, if you want his property, you must wed Ruth too.'

But this (as Boaz clearly anticipated) the anonymous kinsman is not willing to do. 'At this, the kinsman-redeemer said, "Then I cannot redeem it because I might endanger my own estate'" (4:6).

He may simply be saying that the financial burden of two widows was more than he could reasonably afford: 'It would bankrupt me!' Or he might be anticipating problems ahead between his own family and any sons he might give Ruth. One suspects that arguments over title to property were all too common in these lawless days. Wise men probably organized their affairs so as to avoid them. Or it is just possible that his comment reveals an element of superstition. In Genesis 38 there is an interesting story that is not without some parallel to this story of Ruth (and Ruth 4:12 specifically alludes to it). It is the story of Tamar, Judah's daughter-in-law, who was, like Ruth, widowed young. Judah refused to give his son to Tamar according to the levirate law, because he superstitiously thought that there might be a curse on the woman and that he would also lose that son. Some such thought as that may have been going through the kinsman's head. 'Who is to say there isn't a jinx on Ruth? After all, all the men in her family do seem to die in mysterious circumstances. Maybe there's some lethal pagan magic attached to her. She is a Moabitess, after all ...'

For whatever reason, the kinsman is unwilling to assume the legal responsibility of kinsman-redeemer and levirate marriage. So he says to Boaz, 'I am unable to redeem it, you redeem it for yourself.' And Boaz does.

Have you noticed a strange echo in chapter 4 of the situation that prevailed in chapter 1? There it was Ruth and Orpah, you remember, who were faced with a choice: stay with Naomi, or go back to Moab. Orpah, though she felt the pull of family duty to some extent, found the personal cost involved in staying with Naomi more than she was prepared to pay. So she waved Naomi good-bye. She had the right to do it; there was no blame attached to her. The cost of covenant love was just a little bit too much for her. Ruth, on the other hand, was willing to go the extra mile. She stayed. Love, for her, meant sacrificial commitment.

A similar choice now faces these two men. But once again, only one of them is prepared to accept the sacrificial responsibility which covenant love, as defined in God's law, demanded. The other finds the cost too great. 'I can't redeem,' he says. 'I will endanger my own estate if I do. You redeem it for yourself.'

The marriage

Then Boaz announced to the elders and all the people, 'Today you are witnesses that I have bought from Naomi all the property of Elimelech, Kilion and Mahlon. I have also acquired Ruth the Moabitess, Mahlon's widow, as my wife, in order to maintain the name of the dead with his property, so that his name will not disappear from among his family or from the town records. Today you are witnesses!'

Then the elders and all those at the gate said, 'We are witnesses. May the LORD make the woman who is coming into your home like Rachel and Leah, who together built up the house of Israel. May you have standing in Ephratah and be famous in Bethlehem. Through the offspring the LORD gives you by this young woman, may your family be like that of Perez, whom Tamar bore to Judah (4:9–12).

So it is that Naomi, who came back empty from Moab,

finds herself at the end of this story with her lap full not just of corn but full with a grandson, a grandson of whom in her old age she can be proud.

> The women said to Naomi, 'Praise be to the LORD, who this day has not left you without a kinsman-redeemer. May he become famous throughout Israel! He will renew your life and sustain you in your old age. For your daughter-in-law, who loves you and who is better to you than seven sons, has given him birth' (4:14–15).

Seeing the total picture

What does our author want us to learn as this charming and beautifully narrated story ends? As we conclude, let's review the whole story and draw out a number of inter-woven threads.

The role of women in God's purposes

The phrase 'a woman of noble character' in 3:11 is exactly the same as that used in Proverbs 31:10 to describe the noble wife. It may very well be one author quoting the other (which way round depends on one's view of the date of the composition of Ruth). Ancient Israel, of course, was an intensely patriarchal society, and never more so than in the period of the judges when violent male machismo was the established order of the day. Yet in this story we are presented with a woman of independence, self-reliance and courage. True, she uses her feminine wiles, but never, I believe, in a morally unscrupulous way. She does not seek to manipulate Boaz, nor to unfairly entrap him. She does not seduce him or threaten to embarrass him publicly. The interesting thing about Ruth is that she takes the initiative in finding a husband for herself, yet she never compromises her essential femininity in doing so. She does not usurp the man's role. On the contrary, she appeals to Boaz to fulfil his special masculine responsibility as leader in the affair. She does not try to compete with the man, rather she strengthens his arm in doing what deep down he knew he ought to do, and what, deep down perhaps, he knew he wanted to do.

I do not want to labour this point. But in the current ferment about gender, there seems to be a model here that all of us, men and women, could profitably consider. Ruth is most certainly not a passive doormat under a man's feet. But neither is she an aggressive rival to his ego. She does not emasculate him by her feminist ambition, but empowers him by the strong, supportive, moral example of her love.

It may be that women generally understand covenant love and its sacrifices better than men do. I think that is certainly true in a capitalist society, where men are trained to be rivals and competitors. I suspect that I am speaking for most men when I say that the kind of strong, supportive, morally committed love which Ruth exemplifies is what we most need, and most long for, in a wife.

Is saying something like that a capitulation to sexist stereotyping? Is Ruth, for all her courage and nobility, still in this story a victim of the oppressive patriarchy of her culture? Or does the Bible intend her to be a model of godly femininity for all time? I merely pose the question.

The role of the family in social welfare

Both of the ancient laws that undergird the story of Ruth – the law of levirate marriage and the law of redemption – centre on the role of kinship in social welfare.

Our society, at least in recent years, has by its statutes and welfare programmes often had the effect of removing responsibility from the family. Biblical law, by the very structure of its welfare provisions, places responsibility on the family to care for its own. In turn, that meant that people had an enormous economic interest in maintaining strong family connections.

At a time when we are beginning to realize the huge tax cost of a welfare system in a community where family breakdown is almost becoming the norm, this story has, it seems to me, considerable relevance for our legislators. They could profitably reflect on the way in which Old Testament law structured itself in this regard. It is quite pointless to pronounce platitudes about the importance of family life, if we are at the same time stripping the family of its economic and social functions. If we generate a situation in which both parents have to work in order to survive financially, we shall have neglected children and the statistics of youth crime will escalate as a result. If we generate a situation in which families have no room to accommodate their elderly relatives at home, we shall have lonely old people, beds occupied in the hospital that we cannot release, and a demand for geriatric residential homes which then have to be financed. If we generate a situation in which adultery is seen as fun and divorce is unpenalized in the courts, we shall have ever-increasing numbers of fatherless children and the emotional debris that results.

Look at any society, and you will discover that the family is only strong when it is supported by the economic and legal structure of that society. Mere sexual attraction and family affection are not a reliable enough social adhesive on their own to protect family life. The Bible has a lot of wisdom for legislators in this respect.

The openness of God's heart to people of all races

Have you noticed how often the adjective Moabitess is attached to Ruth's name in this story? Almost every time her name is mentioned it is 'Ruth the Moabitess', though the description is quite redundant most of the time.

The reason our author alludes to Ruth's ethnic origin so repeatedly is that he wants to warn his audience not to interpret the covenant of God chauvinistically. The Jews were always prone to do this: 'Aren't we the chosen nation?' Ethnocentricity and racist prejudice were always a danger for them. But throughout the Old Testament there is a strong strand of protest against any kind of xenophobic tendency. Abraham's promise is that he will be the means of blessing to *all* the nations, and Ruth is a classic example of that. She is a Moabitess by birth, but spiritually she is a believer in the God of Abraham. The thrust of our story is that as such, she has as much title to the protection of God's law and to acceptance among God's people as any native-born Jewess.

As Christians, of course, we should not need to be told things like that. But I suspect we do. Eyebrows would no doubt have been raised in Bethlehem at the news that

Boaz was marrying a woman from Moab. Can you imagine the scandal on the street corners as that news was gossiped around? I wonder how other members of his family felt about the move? For you and I know that no matter how liberal we are in theory, no matter how outspokenly anti-racist, it's a different matter when it is our son who wants to marry the black – or white – girl. No. Learn, from the story of Ruth, that God is colour-blind. He really means it when he says he looks on the heart. So, therefore, should we.

A story about love

But most of all, this is a story about love, and the real meaning of love. It's a story designed to deprogramme us from our selfish, individualistic, therapeutic attitude towards love. It's a story that's meant to encourage us to believe that if we really want to know what love means in its fullest and richest form, we must be willing for commitment and sacrifice as the price of love.

Kenneth Clarke comments in his book *Civilization*, 'We can destroy ourselves by cynicism as well as by bombs.' That's a shrewd observation. It's all too easy, when evil is in the ascendant, to become demoralized and pessimistic. Many an idealistic young person surrenders to disillusionment and doubt in mid-life, under the pressures of a world where goodness seems so often to lose out. In some respects that is exactly the danger represented by Naomi in the story. She is a woman of faith, but she is reduced by the devastating impact of family bereavement to a state of stubborn resentment. 'Don't call me Naomi,' she says. 'Call me Mara. The Almighty has made my life bitter.'

Naomi articulates there the complaint of every believer who finds themselves the innocent victim of God's judgment on this fallen world. 'How can you go on believing in the love of God, when things like this happen?' we ask. The world is too miserable, too pain-ridden, too tragic for faith in any God to survive, except a God of ruthless and callous indifference.

But Naomi discovers that her cynicism is misplaced. God is love, and at the end of the day his love will be victorious. How was that faith restored to her? As the result of her personal experience of the human love of Ruth. That's how her faith in the covenant love of the God of Israel was restored; that's how her soul was saved. Because another human being demonstrated such love to her.

If we are going to avoid the perils of cynicism in this broken world of ours, that is how we too must find our faith sustained and how we must seek to sustain the faith of others. In this turbulent period of the judges, it was not the physical heroism of Samson's strength that carried forward the eternal purpose of God. It was the moral heroism of Ruth's love.

How does chapter 4 end?

'Naomi has a son.' And they named him Obed. He was the father of Jesse, the father of David (4:17).

So the little town where it had all happened, Bethlehem, would become famous. Not, as in the past, for pillage and rape; but as the birthplace of kings. And one day, a thousand years on, the King of kings himself would be born there, and Ruth would find special mention in his genealogy in Matthew 1.

Covenant love. Sacrificial love. Redemptive love. Do

we really believe in such love? A love which is not merely the intensity of feeling located in some region between the brain and the groin, but which is a moral commitment to another person?

If we would see the ultimate demonstration of such love, we must look to a cross; a cross where God himself demonstrated the extremity to which covenant love will go, in its commitment and sacrifice, in its determination to redeem the loved one. And from that cross he says to us, 'Love one another, as I have loved you.'